True Crime

True Crime

OBSERVATIONS ON VIOLENCE AND MODERNITY

Mark Seltzer

Routledge
Taylor & Francis Group
New York   London

Routledge is an imprint of the
Taylor & Francis Group, an informa business

Routledge
Taylor & Francis Group
270 Madison Avenue
New York, NY 10016

Routledge
Taylor & Francis Group
2 Park Square
Milton Park, Abingdon
Oxon OX14 4RN

© 2007 by Taylor & Francis Group, LLC
Routledge is an imprint of Taylor & Francis Group, an Informa business

Printed in the United States of America on acid-free paper
10 9 8 7 6 5 4 3 2 1

International Standard Book Number-10: 0-415-97794-0 (Softcover) 0-415-97793-2 (Hardcover)
International Standard Book Number-13: 978-0-415-97794-4 (Softcover) 978-0-415-97793-7 (Hardcover)

Visit the Taylor & Francis Web site at
http://www.taylorandfrancis.com

and the Routledge Web site at
http://www.routledge-ny.com

This book is once more for my son John, who—smart, funny, intelligent, caring boy—knows why, too.

CONTENTS

ACKNOWLEDGMENTS

Versions of several chapters of this book were first published in the journals *Critical Inquiry* and *Trajekte: Zeitschrift des Zentrums für Literaturforschung Berlin* and the collections *After-Images of the City*, editors Joan Ramon Resina and Dieter Ingenschay (Ithaca: Cornell University Press, 2003) and *Violence*, editor Neil L. Whitehead (Santa Fe: School of American Research Press, 2004). I am grateful for permission to allow them to reappear in new form here. This book was written in Berlin and Los Angeles and these cities have left their very different imprints on it. There and here, many colleagues and friends have made their impressions on it: I will not list them—they know who they are.

CHAPTER I

Murder/Media/Modernity

The Media Apriori

True crime has its own weather. Consider, for example, the weather report by which the popular novelist Haruki Murakami opens his nonfiction account *Underground*, a "true picture" of a crime of "overwhelming violence"—the 1995 sarin gas attack on the Tokyo subway system that killed 12 and injured thousands:

> The date is Monday 20 March 1995. It is a beautiful clear spring morning. There is still a brisk breeze and people are bundled up in coats. Yesterday was Sunday, tomorrow is the Spring Equinox, a national holiday. Sandwiched right in the middle of what should have been a long weekend, you're probably thinking "I wish I didn't have to go to work today." No such luck. You get up at the normal time, wash, dress, breakfast, and head for the subway station. You board the train, crowded as usual. Nothing out of the ordinary. It promises to be a perfectly run-of-the-mill day. Until five men in disguise poke at the floor of the carriage with the sharpened tip of umbrellas, puncturing some plastic bags filled with a strange liquid.[1]

This is "normal time" in the world of the new normal: "normal, too normal" in the sense that, in the stock Western, it is "quiet, too quiet." The weather—the residue of nature and the rites of spring—is there in order immediately to give way to second nature: the routine flow of bodies and machines (the body–machine complex) that makes up the workweek. This is the normal time and second nature of mass commuting and "perfectly run-of-the-mill" workdays, transit and work in a society of total mobilization via media technologies, technologies of body and message transport. These are the ordinary days in which "nothing out of the ordinary" is the promise, or terror, of one run-of-the-mill day after another. And hence it is the risk, or promise, of what has been called "the normal accident": the sudden but always imminent, unforeseen, and endlessly previewed shock to the system.[2]

This is the abnormal normality of the world of true crime. That world—and the styles of violence and intimacy, sociality and belief, that make it up—are the subjects of the chapters that follow. True crime is one of the popular genres of the pathological public sphere. It posits stranger-intimacy and vicarious violation as models of sociality. This might be described as a social tie on the model of *referred pain*. And in that true crime is crime fact that looks like crime fiction, it marks or irritates the distinction between real and fictional reality, holding steadily visible that vague and shifting region between truth and falsity where belief resides: what we can call, on the model of referred pain, *referred belief*.

The technical infrastructure of that referred pain and that referred belief today is the mass media. The mass media in the expanded sense make up the psychotechnologies of everyday life in modern society. These are the social and technical systems of body and information transport, commuting and communication—the motion industries and the message industries—that are defining attributes of that society. They make up the reality of the mass media. True crime, a media form of modern self-reflection, at once exposes and effects that reality. The combinations of communication and corporeality, synthetic witnessing, and the media apriori: these together form the working parts of what I will be calling the crime system.

True crime is thus part of our contemporary wound culture, a culture—or at the least, cult—of commiseration. If we cannot gather in the face of anything other than crime, violence, terror, trauma, and the wound, we can at least commiserate. That is, as the novelist Chuck Palahniuk concisely expresses it in his recent novel *Survivor,* we can at least "all [be] miserable together."[3] This is, as it were, the model of nation as support group.

Murakami's account of the attack on the Tokyo underground as mass-public trauma—and as commiseration via the mass media—at once instances that model of nation and crime and parries it. *Underground,* on the face of it, is not exactly, in its form or in its cases in point, typical of true crime. We might say that it turns that typicality inside out, that it turns its cases and its "case-likeness" back on themselves (the alibi—*In Cold Blood* style—of self-exemption through self-reflection). But the point not to be missed is that true crime is always taking exception to itself, always looking over its own shoulder, and by analogy, inviting viewers and readers to do the same. For that reason, a brief sampling of Murakami's account and its semitypicality will make it possible provisionally to take the measure of the world of true crime. More exactly, in that true crime is in effect always taking stock of itself, it will make it possible to locate too, at least initially, how true crime exposes and secures its truth.

"That half of the railway was absolute hell. But on the other side, people were walking to work as usual" (*Underground,* p. 16): there is a double reality to the scenes of violence that make up true crime, made up at once of the event and its registration (or nonregistration). The world of true crime is a self-observing world of observers; the generalization and intensification of that reflexive situation mean that "[t]he registration and revelation of reality make a difference to reality. It becomes a different reality, consisting of itself plus its registration and revelation."[4] Hence, it is not merely a matter of the routine traffic flow interrupted by the usual violent accident. The mass-motion industries, from the start—from railway shock to (here) a media-dependent terrorism—couple violence and its mass observation. There is everywhere a doubling of act and observation, such that public violence and mass death are theater for the living.

The doubling of act and observation has a specific form in true crime: true crime is premised on an inventory of the aftermath and a return to the scene of the crime. It consists, along those lines, in a conjectural reenactment of the crime. That conjectural reenactment takes the form of a probable or statistical realism: "you're probably thinking," "you get up at the usual time," "you board the train," and so on. The known world of true crime is the observed world—and the knowing and observation of that. Forensic realism takes as given, then, the compulsion to observation and self-observation that is a precondition of modernity. This means that forensic observation—conditional and counterfactual—is itself observed as the real work of true crime. Mapping the known world as the scene of the crime, the CNN effect is in effect coupled to the CSI one.

In Los Angeles, among other places, the in-transit eyewitnessing of the everyday accident—what is called the "spectator slowdown"—enters into the radio traffic report that runs (along with the cell phone) as a kind of soundtrack to the commuting between private and public spaces. Hence, the reporting on the event becomes part of, and enters into, the event reported on. (This is no doubt proper for a city in which the traffic jam—along with shopping and the airport queue—is the last folk ritual of social gathering.)

In Murakami's account of the attack on the Tokyo underground system, the event and its witnessing run side by side albeit bypassing each other, even on the part of those who experience it: "'Hey, what's going on here?' but I had to get to work. ... Oddly enough, though, the atmosphere wasn't tense at all. Even I was feeling strange. I'd inhale and no breath would come ... I just caught the next train" (*Underground*, pp. 49–50). It is as if, like the news, witnessing, even self-witnessing, exists as a form of what risk society theorists call "secondhand nonexperience" (and what others, personalizing the media apriori, call trauma).[5]

This is no doubt evident enough; the self-evidence, even banality, of true crime is part of the story. If true crime forms a body of more or less mediocre and clichéd words and images, the point not to be missed is that (as everyone knows) the cliché (what everyone knows to be known) is the sense of the community at its purest. Sarin gas packets wrapped up in the daily papers, left behind amid the crush of newspaper-reading commuters: this version of the violence–media complex would read like really bad fiction if it were not the banal and everyday realism of really bad fact. In Murakami's crime scene investigation, the scene of the crime is a "mass media scenario" (*Underground*, p. 5) and a "media stampede" (p. 15). There is at once the holding steadily visible of the mass media ("I recorded everything") and the intimation of mass media as itself a form of violence ("What I find really scary though is the media. ... It just made me realize just how frightening television is" [p. 134]).

There is a good deal more to be said about this self-parrying of the media within the media and about the ways in which this media reflexivity holds in place what has come to be called reflexive modernity. And there is a good deal more to be said about how horror *in* the media mutates into a horror *of* it. This is nowhere more evident than in the contemporary gothic, a genre that systematically couples the media sponsorship or determination of our situation with an uncanny violence, as if each holds the place of the other. What Murakami here calls "secondary victimization" via the media—a "double violence"—is the precise register of the media apriori in modern violence, its registration and parrying at once (*Underground,* p. 4).

Take the form of Murakami's account: a series of interviews, with minimal commentary: first-person testimonies of the victims, and, subsequently, of the members of the Aum cult (the religious/political group that planned and executed the attacks). In these miniature autobiographies, the individual describes and observes herself. This in turn allows readers, like readers of the novel or viewers of the cinema, to observe that—and to observe too what she does not observe, and thus to engage in self-reflection on that.

It is not merely that the individuals recorded say more than they know (that they have, say, an unconscious). Saying, recording, transcribing, printing, reading—remembering and knowing—are handed over to machines. These technical combinations of communication and corporeality make experience a matter of referred experience ("My dislike of being asked if there are after-effects might itself be a kind of after-effect" [*Underground,* p. 101]). And the handing over of experience to machines becomes its own theme:

> Murakami: *"Was there any kind of reaction because you refused to have a physical relationship with Asahara* [the master of the Aum cult]*?"*

> "I don't know. I lost my memory after that. I underwent electroshock. I still have the scars from the electricity right here. ... I have no idea at what point, and for what reason my memory was erased." (*Underground,* p. 291)

The communication of what cannot be communicated means that the noncommunicable is not exempt from communication but media-induced too. It posits—with a shocking violence registered and erased at once, with a violence, like shock itself, intensified by self-erasure—a media apriori in persons. (It posits the media, say, as the unconscious of the unconscious.)

The coming apart of system and agency in these episodes is italicized by the state of shock but not reducible to it. The model for shock (from at least Freud on) is the railway accident. And the model for the yielding of agency to the machine is (from at least, for example, Zola's murder novel *La Bête humaine* [1890] on) the runaway train. Here things are taken a step further. The underground railway system is a scale model of the modern social system and its infrastructure. The cult is another. These are, in short, working models of the sequestration and self-corroboration of modern society—by which acts, observations, decisions, and outcomes make up the systems that make them up.

The cult is an artificial social system that includes persons as aftereffects of its operations such that the reflection on that looks like an aftereffect too. The Aum cult members inhabit a sequestered microsociety; they occupy positions in a ramifying, self-generating, and self-conditioned bureaucracy—the Ministry of Health, the Chemical Brigade, the Ministry of Science and Technology, the Animation Division, and so on. The terror "cell," like the cult or the scene of the crime, thus condenses and visibilizes the modern social field, an overlit world whose border would be marked by yellow police crime-scene tape.

The direct link between the Aum organization and communication technologies is clear enough. It is visible in the mass marketing of its disciplinary practices (for example, in its video and photographic records of Asahara's supernatural powers, such as his ability to float in the air—visual special effects played to the electronic and print press). And it is visible in its primary business activities (for example, discount sales of personal computers and pirated software). But media-sponsored life here goes deeper. The technologies of Aum Shinrikyo had as their goal, in part, the development of "a mode of communication without any [external] medium" or, more exactly, the "informationalization of the body" such that the body is in effect nothing but an externalization of the media.[6]

The mingling of technologism and esotericism—the occupation of the crossroads between meditation and mediation—is held steadily visible in the technical bureaucratization and militarization of a self-sufficient anti-society. The Aum organization of life and death is shot through by media forms and protocols. This "scale" version of a military media machine is set up as counter to it, to social systems of body and message transport: to an endless everyday life, an eventless commuting, without purpose.[7]

One finds here then, in the media-driven and media-exposed terror underworld, three linked premises of modern life and modern crime that will concern me in the pages that follow. First, there is the intensified turn of interiors, bodies, and acts into communication (the media apriori). Second, there is the sequestration and self-reflection of the contemporary social field (the locked-room model of the world, modeled, above all, in the small closed space of the scene of the crime). And, third, there is the radical entanglement of violence and technical media of information, transmission, and observation (the violence–media complex).

Murakami makes the connection between the modern social system and the crime system, albeit by proxy, by way of quotation. He quotes from the Unabomber manifesto (published by the *New York Times* and the *Washington Post* in April 1995, a month after the sarin attack). In the Unabomber's words,

> The system organizes itself so as to put pressure on those who do not fit in. Those who do not fit into the system are "sick"; so to make them fit in is to "cure." Thus, the power process aimed at attaining autonomy is broken and the individual is subsumed into the other-dependent power process enforced by the system. (Quoted in *Underground,* p. 199)

The Unabomber's scare quotes point to criteria of evaluation ("sick," "cure") that are strictly relative to, and only make sense within, self-induced and self-corroborated systems of valuation (rival "power processes"). This is a snapshot version of a popular sociology and a popular psychology—in that popular sociology and popular psychology are, in effect, sociality and psychology in scare quotes. They are, like the cliché, the quotation of no one in particular, the generalization of a latent, everyday culture sponsored and held in place by the mass media (in this case, the newspapers).

The world in scare quotes indicates the impasse of a way of thinking that has seen through itself but goes on anyway. This is what I call (following Poe, the inaugural true crime writer) the situation of half-belief or "half-credence," the collective idiom of reflexive modernity. That situation of half-credence calls less for an archaeology of knowledge than for what might be called an archaeology of knowingness.

This self-discrediting style of belief is the style of belief proper to the society that makes itself up as it goes along, and whose individuals are compelled to do the same. Modern social systems make themselves from themselves, and in the process generate an archipelago of working models.

These many variants of the bioscript and the educating, correcting, training, grading, and self-realizing institution or associations are, we know, the social microsystems, the small worlds, that calibrate and compare and realize individuals and that lend incremental form to the lifestyle called a career. Here, in these microsocieties, the possibilities of personally attributable action, evaluation, reflection, and belief are distributed.[8] (The sequestration of the academy—the extreme narrowness of its citation circles—provides one ready-to-hand version of that.) Modern society to the extent that it generates and dispels its own criteria of uncertainty, decision, and outcome is, as it were, rereflected in these small worlds, microworlds that model this self-generation and self-conditioning. They are in effect scale models of the modern social field, which is in effect then a life-size model of itself.

This is the case for genre institutions, such as grade schools or 12-step programs, cults or supports groups, the workplace, and self-realization regimes. And it is the case too, then, for those artificial social systems that provide a free trial period for them: genre forms and genre fictions such as true crime and its double, the crime novel.

That is to say, the self-modeling of society is premised on the media doubling of the world. What Murakami's true crime stories set out—the situation of spectation without action, the failure to make application of "the news" to themselves, a training in observation without the pressure or capacity to act or to decide, and the experience of oneself as an aftereffect— is nothing but the presumption of that media doubling of the world.

The world in scare quotes is premised on—as in these cases of crime, cult, and the modern underground system—an everyday intimacy with the systems of things that come and go, vanish and return, on schedule, like newspapers or trains or commuters. This is what I will be calling (following the crime writing of Patricia Highsmith) the sociality of those who walk away, the media-sponsored intimacy, for example, of strangers on trains who listen or view, commiserate, and forget.

The model for this—for the self-conditioning and self-corroboration of events, evaluations, and ends in its media reflection—is the novel itself. That is one reason why I take many of my examples from the novel. The novel provides the field manual for the autopoietic, or self-making, conditions of the modern social system (and then gives itself an aesthetic self-exemption from them). This is nowhere more evident than in the crime novel, where the possibilities for decision and indecision, plan and counterplan, self-delusion and self-disclosure, are socially distributed, individualized, and mapped in high relief. And it is nowhere more compelling, nowhere more compulsively or rigorously systematized, than in the cult genre of true crime, which knowingly takes the crime novel as its prototype and tries it out on real life.

Synthetic Witnessing

In true crime—the scene of the crime, the media apriori in persons, its electroshock effects—one finds, localized and pathologized, the shock modernity recoils from in its own realization. One finds too the mass witnessing of these effects, which is, in the case of Murakami, among others, a witnessing of witnesses. Witnessing self-witnessing—and the self-conditioned deconstruction of both—has been a proof test of the media of real life since the eighteenth-century novel, from Samuel Richardson's *Pamela* (the phrase "real life" was first used by the eighteenth-century printer, model letter writer, and novelist Richardson) to *The Bachelorette*. Here the modern compulsion to observation—self-observation and mass observation—is itself staged and observed in the contemporary and popular genre of the *spokesvictim*.

That focus on individual description (the interview and the self-interview) is part of true crime's mode of operation and part of its strange attraction. One finds here (as in witness literature more generally) a compulsive self-description. Stated very generally, modern crime and modern violence—that is, the mass-mediated spectacle of torn bodies and torn persons—provide points of crystallization for the intensified relays of bodies and the technical media in contemporary life.

For one thing, the manner in which the event thus takes the form of its observation and self-observation fuses the media apriori and the social compulsion that requires self-describing individuals:

> The nature of modern society doubtless makes it seem obvious to presuppose second order observation in all communication. This is true with regard to the attribution of communication to individuals, whose individuality in the modern view consists precisely in this individual observing himself as an observer and not simply living his life.[9]

If the unobserved life, on this view, is not worth living, then living one's life cannot be separated from its media doubling.

For another, "ethically objectionable acts must have victims."[10] Hence, the spectacle of violent crime provides a point of attraction and identification, an intense individualization of these social conditions, albeit a socialization via the media spectacle of wounding and victimization. To the extent that action, like motive, must be attributed to individuals, these small and intense melodramas of the wound acclimatize readers and viewers to take these social conditions personally. These social conditions then, in turn, take on the form of a pathological public sphere.

In wound culture, act and motive take the form of the *case* or *case history*, an act conscripted by a norm. As Murakami expresses it, his attempt to work through the "Tokyo gas attack and the Japanese psyche" aimed at this:

What were the people in the subway carriages doing at the time? What did they see? What did they feel? What did they think? If I could, I'd have included details on each individual passenger, right down to their heartbeat and breathing, as graphically represented as possible. The question was, what would happen to any ordinary Japanese citizen—such as me or any of my readers—if they were suddenly caught up in an attack of this kind? (*Underground*, p. 196)

That is, the intense individualization of these accounts by interview is coupled with an intensive anonymization and systematization, any ordinary citizen or reader, anatomized "as graphically as possible." The double logic of the "graphic"—vividly lifelike and diagrammatic at once—is the logic of the case.[11]

Here we might take as a case in point the cover image of the American edition of *Underground:* a map of the Tokyo underground network superimposed on a male torso. The subway system, more precisely, is superimposed on an anatomical drawing of the musculatory and circulatory systems opened to view beneath the skin. The system map takes the place of the lungs, and a series of entrance arrows mark the intake route (a line drawing in place of mouth and throat) to the body's interior. It is not quite then that a machine system has invaded the body. The system beneath the skin and the transit system, anatomy and the media, meet and fuse, two interpenetrating systems, each transparent to the other—the coordinate geometry of the body–machine complex.

Here we might consider too the recurrent tendency of the victims interviewed to see the event not as a terrorist act but instead as an accident: they "just happened to be gassed on their way to work" (*Underground*, p. 41); "had I died, I probably could have accepted it in my own way as just a kind of accident" (*Underground*, p. 44); "it feels more like I had an accident" (*Underground*, p. 51), and so on. On the logic of the accident, the victim of the sarin attack is a statistical victim, one of an indeterminate number of others, a victim of the law of large numbers.

If the constitutive feature of act, like motive, is that it must be attributed to individuals, then the self-experience of act as accident conserves individuality ("in my own way") by negation. Otherwise, living one's life as a matter of deciding one's individuality for oneself—setting one-self in motion, reflecting on it, and in doing so realizing oneself—would give way to a merely statistical individuality. And act and motive—most graphically, criminal acts and motives—would enter into a social calculus of probability at the expense of persons and their acts and motives (see Chapter 3, "The Crime System") or, as one victim puts it, make visible "[j]ust how weak the individual is" (*Underground*, p. 57). All acts and motives would be locked into a "world machine."[12]

This is nowhere clearer than in the part of life that centers Murakami's interviews: "I would ask the interviewees about ... their job (especially their job)" (*Underground*, p. 6). This special emphasis becomes progressively intelligible. If what the media apriori looks like forms one side of Murakami's version of true crime, what work looks like forms the other. The point not to be missed is that work and the media here are the two sides of a single formation, opposed on part of their surface but communicating on another level.

The true crime world is a mass-observed world: the observation of violence directed against bodies and persons. But the work world, seen this way, is already about a violence against bodies and persons. This is not merely because the attack murders and wounds commuters getting to work; it is also because of the manner in which it exposes the compulsion of a work drive that resembles—in the media automatisms of act, motion, the life process itself, that is,—a death drive: "After Korakuen [station] it got more and more suffocating ... I began to think, 'I'll never make it to work today'" (*Underground*, p. 99); "My main thought was, 'I can't be late for work.' Of course I felt bad about leaving people just lying there on the platform, but it was an important day for me so the pressure was on not to be late" (*Underground*, p. 122); "That's when I knew I'd breathed the gas. 'I'd better call the office,' I thought ... 'There's been some terrorist activity. I'm going to be late'" (*Underground*, p. 183); "Whereas most people, although *they* were in a bad way physically, still tried to get to work somehow ... in fact, one guy near me was crawling!" (*Underground*, p. 133).

Work—self-fulfilling work, therapeutic working through, recreational working out—making it to work is bound up through and through with the unremitting drill in the work of modern self-making, in which body and nature know their place.[13] The greater number of the victims interviewed are "salary men," the often highly self-ironized Japanese version of the white-collar worker: "Once out of college I became your typical salaryman" (*Underground,* p. 182). And, on the logic of a work ethic conscripted by the new corporate ethos (a world machine), "[W]hat choice does a salaryman have" (p. 96). Murakami's account then might be seen as part of that large literature devoted to diagnosing the torn emotional life of middle managers, the life of the organization man, the man in the gray-flannel suit, the life of "office-dwelling hominids": "Their true social life is the office," as the contemporary novelist J. G. Ballard puts it; the office is "their key psychological zone."[14]

We know that what is alternatively called "the control revolution," "the second industrial revolution," and the emergence of the "information society" involved a basic transformation in work and the workplace. We know too that the real achievement of the managerial and control revolution was not the invention of a system of industrial discipline (that system extended throughout the social body from the late eighteenth century on). The innovation of the control revolution was the redescription of managerialism, supervision, and observation, in the idiom of production. That is, the real innovation becomes visible in the incorporation of the representation and observation of the work process into the work process itself or, better, the incorporation of the representation and observation of the work process *as the work process itself.*

To the extent that this transformation is popularly seen as the replacement of real persons, real bodies, and real work by their representation and observation—to the extent that the new world of work is popularly seen as a way of doing away with bodies and persons—the generalization of observation and its technical media looks itself something like a crime. At the same time, the real work of observation and the reality of the mass media, derealized as the opposite of real work, can then remain unobserved. The media presumption of reflexive modernity is, in the genre of true crime as in its codependent crime fiction, at once generalized and pathologized, hence acclimatizing readers and viewers to it and self-exempting them from it at once. That is to say, the media apriori—as in Poe's "The Purloined Letter," his inaugural story of the exact coincidence of detective work and the technical media (in this case, the letter)—seems "a little too self-evident" to be seen.

For the moment, it is possible less to explain this complex of media, work, and violence than to exemplify it. Take, for example, the popular media in which the scene of the crime and the new world of work are drawn into an absolute proximity, such that each includes the other. In, for example, the ramifying franchise television show *CSI,* city by city mapping the virtual nation as crime scene, the scene of the crime is not merely an information-processing zone.[15] Like *ER,* the most popular television program before it, *CSI* is premised on the work-centered life, and along with that, and defining that, the endless spectacle of a series of torn and opened bodies that define a wound culture and the technical processing of torn and opened bodies that define the body–machine complex—with the difference that in *CSI* observation replaces act; the only real work is the work of observation via machines. Body processing and information processing become two ways of doing the same thing, via the stylish thrill of a media-saturated workplace, with great appliances and a pretty good soundtrack.

CSI is, of course, *crime scene investigation*—the acronym, as with PTSD, ADHD, or OCD in the *DSM,*[16] indicating that expert, professional work is going on, that it has located its "object"—and black-boxed it. The black box here is the crime scene itself, the ritualized demarcation of physical space as information zone and the technical processing of physical evidence, which is nothing but that which can be technically processed. The technical media determine the situation, allowing the moral neutrality of the media technician itself to be moralized. *CSI* is not interested in law (which is full of lawyers) and not interested in psychology (which is full of psychologists and talk show hosts). The media phenomenon of *CSI* is interested in the perfect functioning of the media. That provides the extreme test of the reality of the mass media: the crime system and the media doubling of act and observation double each other. The media dictates its own content—here, that bodies and persons are processed in its own terms, and that there is nothing "deeper" than that.

The real social life of these workers is the office and laboratory world, and the media-saturated workplace is their key psychological zone. Outside of their workplace, there is nothing but torn bodies and torn lives.

Inside it, recollections of the workers' past lives (the sex and intimacy that preceded what amounts to a posthumous life in forensics) and reconstructions of the victims' past lives (reconstructed as machinic life).

The return to the scene of the crime takes the technical form of the conjectural reenactment (the counterfactual flashback). It takes the form, along with that, of a strictly material and technical reconstruction of bodies and acts (a technics of observation, and bioscripting, via trauma-processing machines). There is, in short, in this work nothing but the work of observation and self-observation—and, of course, the mass-media viewing of that: *the mass observation of the work of observing, at the center of the murder leisure industry.*

The policy of conjectural reenactment makes another and crucial contribution to the mass media's cultural institutionalization of what acts and actors look like. The postmortem body centers the *CSI* episode; on the autopsy table, we know, forensics and pornography meet and fuse.[17] Here too—in the piece-by-piece reassembly of bodies and acts and the reattachment of both to actors—acts and persons are put back together.

The typical true crime account imitates the opening of the classic crime novel: it typically opens with a brief factual summary of the case, something like a bare press release on the event and scene. And this is the scene to which the novel then returns and proceeds to narrate in an extended aftermath. True crime stories, like the classic murder novel, begin at the end and proceed to reconstruct both motive and act, returning both to single actors.[18]

True crime, like crime fiction, singles out acts and actors, and rejoins bodies and intentions, torn bodies and interior states, that have come apart. But it is not merely that the crime story makes acts, choices, and consequences luridly explicit and explicitly consequential. It makes explicit how difficult it is—given the double contingency or overdetermination of motives, causes, and effects in modern social systems—to single them out (to ascribe them to individuals who are then individualized through that ascription). The mass media today at once performs this function and displays it:

The media favour attributing things to action, that is, to actors. Complex background circumstances which might have motivated, if not coerced, an actor to do what he or she did cannot be fully illuminated. ... [Following Weber, it may be recalled that] neither actions nor actors are given as empirical facts. The boundaries (and therefore the unity) of an action or of an actor cannot be seen nor heard. In each case, what we are dealing with are institutionally and culturally congruent constructs.[19]

Hence the retroactive constructs of true crime—by which causes and motives are reattached to the effects of acts (the torn body). This is what it looks like to recombine effects and causes, bodies and psychologies—and, therefore, to refer acts back to persons. The true crime show performs the public service of locating individuals—finding missing persons—albeit via a generalization of the scene of the crime as the boundaries of the modern social field.

True and False Crime

True crime is crime fact that looks like crime fiction. If one goes into a chain bookstore today, one will find a large section of books called "crime" and a much smaller one called "true crime." The large section consists of crime fiction; the second consists of crime fact. This is crime fact of a specific kind: a species of paperback sociology that, for the most part, retells real-life cases of crime. But these popular real-life case histories do so following the conventions of popular crime fiction.

"Crime" on its own is then crime fiction, "false crime." The presumption seems to be that "crime" is a fictional genre and that one must bend fiction toward fact by adding the word "true" to crime. This interestingly paradoxical relation between true and false crime points to the manner in which crime in modern society resides in that interval between real and fictional reality—that is, the uncertain and mobile, conditional, and counterfactual, reality of a "reflexive modernity," a modernity that includes the self-reflection of its reality as part of its reality, and as one of its defining attributes. That is, a reality bound up through and through with the reality of the mass media.

Put somewhat differently, true crime points to the media apriori in modern society. This is because the technical infrastructure of modern reflexivity is the mass media. It points to the fact that the real world is known through its doubling by machines, the doubling of the world in the mass media that makes up our situation.

The known world today is a mass-mediated one. But to the very extent that the known world is known via the media (to the very extent that it can be known, and known to be known about, only via the mass media), real life seems to yield to its fictionalization (or to what is euphemized as the "social construction of reality").

In the accounts of true crime that follow, I move between crime fiction and crime fact. This is not because there is no distinction between them but because the distinction between them is everywhere in play within them. That is the case from Poe's crime fiction, saturated with factual newspaper accounts, to Patricia Highsmith's novels about a violence bound to a media rivalry, a media rivalry that includes, among other things, novels.

The presumption of a reflexive relation between crime fact and fiction is never in doubt in "classic" true crime. Here we might instance the extensive writings of William Roughead, who, from 1889 to 1949, attended every high-profile murder trial held in the High Court in Edinburgh, and published a series of best-selling accounts of them (a criminological graphomania that captured the attention of the general public and of fiction writers such as Henry James). There is everywhere, in the doubling of these cases in writing, a double focus on act and media, this not least in that the question of motive is often bound to the question of media sensation ("she did not commit the crime for the sake of notoriety") and to the "ebullition of public feeling" in the "public prints" ("the inexhaustible persistence of a public spirited and resourceful Press! Word of her release 'transpired'; speedily she was pursued, run to earth, and taken captive by enterprising journalists in quest of copy").[20] There is, internal to the cases, an ongoing comparison of fact and fiction ("to compare her story of the crime with the facts established at the trial . . . will furnish an intellectual pastime more entertaining and worthier the effort than the solving of many cross-word puzzles" [*Classic Crime*, p. 259]). There is, internal to the cases, the entry of fiction into the interior of the crime (for example, in case of the impostor and "double-dealing" thief Deacon Brodie, whose "histrionic tastes" and identification with literary rogues—his "Macheath complex"—were remodeled in turn in Stevenson's *Strange Story of Dr. Jekyll and Mr. Hyde* [*Classic Crime*, pp. 43–44]). There is a commutability of murder and writing ("it was the best murder he had ever read" [p. 218]). And these easy transitions from fact to fiction and back ("someone has since made a fiction out of the old facts" [p. 260]) mean that the mass media emerges as its own theme ("the report of the trial extended to 173 columns . . . contained 52,000 words, and the verbatim report 346,000 … the total number of words telegraphed from Edinburgh in connection with the case was 1,860,000" [p. 861]).

I have elsewhere taken up this commutability of word counts and body counts, and its implications. And it will be necessary to take up the exact coincidence of the autonomy of modern crime—what Roughead calls "mischief for mischief's sake"—and the autonomy of modern art (an art for art's sake that provides the model for murder as one of the fine arts).[21] But my sampling of the relays between fact and fiction that center true crime is, for the moment, directed somewhat differently. It is by way of giving some indication of the sheer banality and utter conventionality of the genre's self-deconstruction; the reflexivity of true crime—the self-organization and self-reflection of its own plausibility—is never in doubt, which indicates that its media apriori is never in doubt either.[22]

Literacy Tests

"Eunice Parchman killed the Coverdale family because she could not read or write." This, the opening sentence of popular murder writer Ruth Rendell's novel *A Judgement in Stone* (1977), makes absolutely explicit the popular understanding of modern crime: the presumption that the question of criminality and the question of the media are two sides of the same formation. Here are the next two sentences: "There was no real motive and no premeditation. No money was gained and no security."[23] Modern crime is motiveless crime in the sense that its motivation is strictly internal and phantasmatic. Modern crime makes itself from itself—and that is the autopoietic (self-making and systemic) style of crime proper to the auto-poietic society, a society that makes itself from itself, on its own terms.

There is a direct connection between the presumption of a media apriori in crime and this ordinance of motives. Here the fact of literacy, or the exclusion from it, makes personhood a function of the media—in this case, reading and print; the fact of literacy, the interest in reading, is both the condition of individualization and the condition of the interest in individualization. Modern crime fiction and true crime, from the 1830s on, is premised on the manner in which reading had become a "necessity of existence."[24] If the modern individual is one who observes his or her own observing, the new self-observing world was "the new 'reading world.'"[25] Or, as another novelist expressed it toward the end of the nineteenth century, "All civilization comes through literature now. ... [W]e must read or we must barbarize."[26] In Rendell's narrator's insistently clichéd terms, "Literacy is one of the cornerstones of civilization" (*Judgement*, p. 1)

But if the media then reveal us to ourselves, how understand this operation of self-revelation by media proxy? The murderer's illiteracy exempts, at a stroke, the reader from complicity in crime—since the act of reading excludes the reader (as reader) from not merely the act and the motive for it but also from the understanding of either. In this media-saturated novel, intimacy and sociality both are understood as effects of shared life via media proxies, what Rendell calls *vicarious life*. The relays between vicarious life and what I will be calling *vicarious crime* turn out to be crucial here.[27]

If the subject of the media is thus individualized via vicarious life, it is not hard to see that that situation unfolds a series of paradoxes. The narrator's cliché-driven narrative makes that exorbitantly visible; the narrative often reads as if *Bartlett's Familiar Quotations* were time-sharing her voice and her mind.[28] For if all civilization is seen to come from literature now, or then, it will be recalled that early print culture—the early modern novel, for example—endlessly rehearsed the dangers to behavior as a consequence of print and the style of deviance and criminality that goes with it.[29]

This means that the novel is not exactly a reflection of the self-conditioning of act, evaluation, and outcome—the universalization of self-reflexivity—that marks the "sequestration" of modern forms of life (the second modernization or reflexive modernity). The novel is not exactly a reflection of that self-corroboration in that, from the later eighteenth century on, it has been a dress rehearsal for it.

Rendell's fiction proceeds by imitating the (fiction-imitating) form of true crime. The novel opens with a brief summary of the actors and scene of the crime (miming a newspaper account, with all its "human interest" clichés). And the novel then goes on to flesh out the bare bones of the plot (retroactively adding psychology, intentions, relations, a childhood, motives, and so on). The plot pivots on something like a literacy test:

> The magazine on the table intimidated [Eunice] as much as a spider might have intimidated another woman. … "Oh, I think it's fun." Melinda turned the page. "Here's a questionnaire. *Twenty Questions to Test If You're Really in Love.* I must do it, though I know I am. Now, let's see. Have you got a pencil or a pen or something?" (*Judgement,* pp. 130–131)

The exposure of Eunice's illiteracy (and its murderous consequences) thus takes the form of a test of mass-media literacy. The questionnaire tests out the credibility of a media-sponsored love. This is a matter of "entertaining" beliefs: the half-credences of no one in particular, recited, seen through, and installed as the referred beliefs one sort of believes ("I must do it, though I know I am"). These are referred beliefs that everyone else like oneself holds: temporary positions that may be occupied for a time before moving on to the next—rehearsed, communicated, and forgotten, with the turning of a page.

The standard bioscript of reflexive modernity standardizes a multiple-choice outlook on life: "But he realized the difficulty of finding an American who (a) had a flat or a house in Venice and (b) would be Bohemian enough to take in a stranger. … [H]e must take up the pieces of his life again. He could make a list of four or five."[30] These are the play-at-home versions of the self-educating and self-realizing microsociety, with all the paradoxes of its self-transparent knowingness.[31]

One consequence of the multiple-choice outlook on life is not hard to detect. The individual does not know who he is because he must decide that for himself; this is the individual who winds himself up to see where he goes. That means that his "determinations must be recognizable as self-determinations," and thus must be made visible and observable.[32] Along these lines, identity is transformed into its communication—that is, at once made visible and exposed as perhaps nothing but its communication.

The multiple-choice effect makes decisions visible; the intense anatomization of individual acts in true and false crime singularizes action; and the observed and self-observed resolution of the act finalizes it. This is what Erving Goffman, writing on "where the action is" in modern mass-mediated life, describes as the "fatefulness" in the manufacture and distribution of "vicarious experience" through the media:

> Fatefulness involves a play of events that can be initiated and real-ized in a space and time small enough to be fully witnessed. Unlike such phenomena as the rise of capitalism or World War II, fate-fulness is something that can be watched and portrayed in toto, from beginning to end at one sitting; unlike these other events, it is inherently suited to watching and to portraiture.[33]

The point not to be missed is that this "vicarious contact" is thus the means by which a "frame of reference is secured for judging daily acts, without having to pay its penalties."[34] The vicarious experience of action, such that act and witnessing, event and media spectacle, indicate each other at every point—this play of events is nowhere more intensely realized and secured than in true and false crime.

We are by now thoroughly familiar with the spectacle of the multiple-choice outlook on life and the transformation of identity and act into communication.[35] After all, this is the terrain of the popular media from the realist novel to reality TV. The crime novel and true crime make these literacy tests as explicit as possible. After all too, the stakes of the test—the staging of the choice of love or money, life or death—could not be more explicit, more urgent, or more generic and self-discrediting; if we must read or view, or we must barbarize, then barbarity—accelerating violence, crimes against humanity—appears as the antidote to the reality of the mass media. The media solicitation of violence as alternative to the media apriori thus returns as its own topic: *Welcome to the desert of the Real!*[36]

Crimes against Humanity

It is as if each successive media technology is reimagined as a reservoir of the humanity it was initially seen to endanger. The individualization of oneself in writing was, after all and from the start, also the compromise of oneself in writing (the betrayal of secrets, including one's own, in print). The media condition of individuality can, from the start then, get in the way of that individuality.[37]

This is in part because new media technologies become visible in terms of what I have elsewhere called a double logic of prosthesis (technology as at once self-extension and self-extinction).[38] New technologies are first experienced in the idiom of pathology and wounding. The typewriter, for example, was, we know, originally designed for the blind, and the telephone was designed to supplement hearing loss. This intimate and paradoxical relation of personhood to the technical media—media-sponsored interiority—makes for the melodramas of uncertain agency that run through these technoir woundscapes and these communities of risk and danger (and this not least in the violent reassertions of that media-sponsored and media-endangered singularity).

That is to suggest that it is not merely that the reality of the known world is the reality of the mass media, in true crime as in other genres of modernity's self-reflection. There is a deeper relation between crime and the media apriori. The known world—the world known and known to be known about (and thus, via its collective communication, making up social reality)—is bound to the technical media. But to the very extent that the known world is indissociable from its media situation, the reality and credibility of the known world seems imperiled. It is, as we say in the risk society, "everywhere at risk." And to the very extent that reality seems at risk, the media apriori in modern crime and modern violence seems itself a form a violence and a kind of crime. This misapprehension of the media (a lethal misapprehension, it will be seen) is a version of what Jean Baudrillard calls *the perfect crime:* the mass-media murder of reality, without a trace. On the logic of this misapprehension, violent crime comes to be seen as, and comes perversely to promise, a return to the real. Modern crime and the modern mass media, vicarious crime and vicarious life, thus include each other—and the media apriori appears in itself as a crime against humanity.

True crime is premised on that double contingency of violence and the media. In the chapters that follow, I want step-by-step to unfold—and to progressively reframe—these premises. I mean to proceed not by surveying the genre of true crime (although I set out some of its conventions) and not exactly by isolating its elementary particles (which are necessarily constituents of the second, reflexive, modernity generally). I mean to proceed by testing—across cases of crime fact (from a murder case in Arkansas to Berlin as the scene of the crime of the century) and crime fiction (particularly Poe and Highsmith)—how true and false crime work.[39] The intent, in short, is to trace the relays among murder, media, and modernity that make up the crime system.[40] And it will become clear how the crime system makes it possible to pressure these accounts. Modern crime, to the extent that it is modern, is premised on the double contingency of murder and the media. Intimations of the media everywhere enter into the crime system—and, in doing so, renovate our situation and the manner in which it becomes observable, compelling, and credible.

The Known World

Juan José Saer's remarkable novel *The Witness* tells two stories at once: a story of the European conquest of America around 1500 and a story of its witnessing. The "witness," as a young boy, had voyaged to the New World and been taken captive, or taken in, by a tribe of Indians, and then sent back after 10 years. Having returned to Europe, and, after performing his "status as real-life survivor" in a series of popular plays devoid of anything like real life, the unnamed narrator becomes a self-isolated man of letters.[41] And, a half century after his return from the experience of a devastated new world that remains his real world, he turns to writing about it, not least "to make real with his quill" those now-vanished people (*Witness*, p. 59).

For Saer, the matter of the conquest is the story of its witnessing, and the matter of witnessing the story of observation and self-observation in writing. That shift from act to observation, and the doubling of both in writing, is by now familiar enough. It is one of the markers of modernity and its self-reflection or theorization. It also indicates the manner in which Saer's novel of the conquest (whatever its accuracy about that) is a story of the modern media, and, more exactly, of the synthetic witnessing via what might be described as the media of modern violence.

The name the witness is given by the Indians (a name that he does not understand, since it seems to stand for many things) is "def-ghi." The name he is given, that is, is a sequence of letters—in effect, the common name of the alphabetization of the world. "The exemplary history of the conquest of America," it has been observed, "teaches us that Western civilization has conquered, among other reasons, because of the superiority in human communication."[42] But if technical superiority in communication (writing) was one among other things that made for the conquest, it was then not, on this account, just one thing among others; the conquest of America, on this view, was the first modern media war (which is to say, both the first modern war and the advent of modernity).

The doubling of reality in writing is here the premise of conquest and witnessing both. A new world of writing and print developed and intensified the possibilities of social communication without interaction; the modern world is a new world that includes its technical self-reflection as part of its reality.[43] That reflexivity is then irreducible to the self-consciousness that is its individualized correlate. The narrator-witness writes "to carry the news of that annihilation" (*Witness*, p. 145). And, to the extent that the annihilation cannot be separated from a superiority in communication, the doubling and exteriorization of the world in "the news" is also the news it carries.

The exteriorization of the world in writing is set against an observed incapacity for that self-observation; the premodern world is seen as subject to "the uncertain fascination of the visible" (*Witness*, p. 74) and the dubious reality of things that move and vanish, things that they had "no way of verifying from outside" (p. 131). It is subject to the "additional uncertainty of not knowing what the universe thought of itself" (p. 131). For the witness, then, this is an unreflective world utterly dependent on its externalized observation by an "outsider"; collaterally, then, its reality is utterly dependent on an unremitting witnessing that holds the world in place and thus takes its place. For the outsider-witness, the violence he observes is thus a violence oriented entirely toward its public witnessing.

Saer's story of the violence of the conquest and its witnessing is also then a fable of the media. The known world is the media world and, knowing what the world thinks of itself, the observation that holds the world together, the media doubling of the world. It posits a witnessing of violence that at once solicits and memorializes it (what Murakami calls the mass media's "double violence").

It is not for the moment a matter of periodizing that modernity but of observing that what one means by modernity, and how one periodizes it, cannot then be separated from its media forms. If this looks like media determine our situation (a media determinism) and if it looks like a sub-jection of sociality to its forms of communication (the system of society), it also points to the experience of that technical self-extension as a form of self-annihilation, as a crime against humanity. And hence it points to the solicitation of the real violence that will undo that; as one corporate logo has it, "all but war is simulation."[44] The public scene is the scene of the crime, and an obsessive observation takes on the ethicized aura of witnessing (along with a new class of professional mourners). Carrying the news to the outside becomes the special providence of the mass media; the uncertain fascinations of the visible, the fugitive reality of things that move, vanish, and regularly return, become the everyday compulsion of the motion industries and the leisure ones (the reality of motion pictures, for example).[45]

It is usual to see this media witnessing as a kind of parasitism (one that we are more or less at home with from the surrogate sensualities of novel reading on). And it is possible to indict the synthetic witnessing of violence in the mass media as nothing but spectator slowdowns:

Disgust at collective killing is of very recent date and should not be overestimated. Today everyone takes part in public executions through the newspapers. Like everything else, however, it is more comfortable than it was. We sit peacefully at home and, out of a hundred details, can choose those to linger over which offer a special thrill.[46]

But the mistake, again, is to understand observing as the opposite of real work and media observation as the opposite of "the real world" in the name of it. It may be that in modern societies "the difference between private and public is temporalized and transformed into the difference between leisure and work."[47] But the difference between leisure and work—and between private and public life—is transformed in the burgeoning systems of observation and self-observation that more and more define both. These transformations are part of the strange attraction of the murder leisure industry (the media apriori that is the subject and form of true crime). They enter into the formation of a pathological public sphere and its infrastructure (the psychotechnologies of everyday life that make up the known world). They point to how the crime system and the system of modern society work, and work together (the relays between crime and modernity that I take up in the chapters that follow).

Notes

1. Haruki Murakami, *Underground: The Tokyo Gas Attack and the Japanese Psyche*, trans. Alfred Birnbaum and Philip Gabriel (London: Harvill Press, 2001), 7. Subsequent references, hereafter abbreviated *Underground,* in parentheses within text.
2. Charles Perrow, *Normal Accidents: Living with High-Risk Technologies* (Princeton, NJ: Princeton University Press, 1999).
3. Chuck Palahniuk, *Survivor* (New York: Random House, 1999), 278.
4. Dirk Baecker, "The Reality of Motion Pictures," *MLN: Modern Language Notes* 111, no. 3 (1996): 560–577.
5. See Ulrich Beck, *Risk Society: Toward a New Modernity,* trans. Mark Ritter (London: Sage, 1992).
6. See Masachi Osawa, "Why Did Aum Use Sarin?" in *Gendai* (October 2005), cited in Shujiro Yazawa, *Japanese Social Movements since World War*

II (Boston, MA: Beacon Press, 1997); Manuel Castells, *The Information Age: Economy, Society, and Culture*, vol. 11: *The Power of Identity* (Oxford: Blackwell, 2004), 100–107. See also Christopher Drew, "Japanese Sect Tried to Buy U.S. Arms Technology, Senator Says," *New York Times*, October 31, 1995, A5.

7. Shinji Miyadai, *Owarinaki Nichijo of Ikiro* [Live in Endless Everyday Life] (Tokyo: Chikuma-Shobo, 1995), cited in Castells, *The Information Age*, 107.

8. See Niklas Luhmann, *The Reality of the Mass Media,* trans. Kathleen Cross (Stanford, CA: Stanford University Press, 2000), 86–87.

9. Niklas Luhmann, *Risk: A Sociological Theory,* trans. Rhodes Barrett (London: Transaction, 2005), 228.

10. Mary Douglas, *Risk Acceptability According to the Social Sciences* (New York: Russell Sage Foundation, 1985), 11.

11. Here it may be recalled that "case" derives from and remains linked to *casus* or *fall,* and that the fallen person or body is the model for becoming a statistic (the statistical person).

12. See Niklas Luhmann, *Social Systems,* trans. John Bednarz Jr. (Stanford, CA: Stanford University Press, 1995), 558.

13. "More and more, work enlists all good conscience on its side," as Nietzsche expressed it in "Leisure and Idleness"; "the desire for joy already calls itself a 'need to recuperate' and is beginning to be ashamed of itself. 'One owes it to one's health'—that is what people say when they are caught on an excursion into the country." Friedrich Nietzsche, *The Gay Science,* trans. Josefine Nauckhoff (Cambridge: Cambridge University Press, 2001).

14. J. G. Ballard, *Super-Cannes* (London: Flamingo, 2001), 93. The Aum cult members inhabit a parallel bureaucratic zone: modern workplace and cult mirror each other, such that "the system" is at once exposed (universalized) and criminalized (delimited).

15. My thanks to Mark McGurl and Sianne Ngai for sharing some of the reasons why they watch *CSI.*

16. These are, respectively: posttraumatic stress disorder, attention deficit with hyperactivity disorder, obsessive–compulsive disorder, and the *Diagnostic and Statistical Manual of Mental Disorders.*

17. This is exactly the center of Zola's advent modern murder novel, *Thérèse Raquin* (1867), a novel that puts in place many of the components of modern "motiveless" crime and its mediascapes. The centering scene of the novel is the public morgue, a scene of publicness fusing the pornographic and the forensic: "Every morning when he was there he could hear the public coming and going behind him. The Morgue is a spectacle within the reach of

every purse, something which passers-by, rich and poor, can enjoy for nothing. The door is open; anyone who wishes to walk in can do so. There are connoisseurs who go out of their way not to miss a single one of these morbid sights. When the slabs are bare, people go away disappointed, feeling they have been swindled and muttering between their teeth. When they are well covered with a fine display of human flesh, the visitors jostle each other for cheap thrills, exclaiming in horror and joking, applauding, or whistling as if they were at the theatre, and go away well satisfied, declaring that the Morgue has certainly put on a good show for the day." Emile Zola, *Thérèse Raquin,* trans. Andrew Rothwell (1868; repr. Oxford: Oxford University Press, 1992), 76. The morgue scene and its gathering of passersby is a prototypicalization of the pathological public sphere convened around spectacles of violence and the wound. Not surprisingly, the Paris public morgue closed around the time the first movie theaters opened there. See Vanessa R. Schwartz, *Spectacular Realities: Early Mass Culture in Fin-de-Siècle Paris* (Berkeley: University of California Press, 1998), 45–88.

18. The burgeoning of the true crime genre has meant that crime fiction, the prototype of true crime, has itself turned to imitate its imitation. I will be looking at, in a moment, one such case in point: Ruth Rendell's novel *A Judgement in Stone.*

19. See Luhmann, *The Reality of the Mass Media,* 32–33. For an account closely related to the analyses of action and evaluation and the conditions of reflexive modernity articulated in social systems theory and modernization theory, but referred to the Benthamite logic of utilitarianism, see Frances Ferguson, *Pornography, the Theory: What Utilitarianism Did to Action* (Chicago: University of Chicago Press, 2004).

20. William Roughead, *Classic Crimes: A Selection from the Works of William Roughead* (New York: New York Review Books, 2000), 214, 259. Hereafter abbreviated *Classic Crime.*

21. See chapter 5, "Vicarious Crime."

22. The novelization of real crimes has, of course, a long history (the history of the novel, for instance). And the novelists Truman Capote (*In Cold Blood*) and Norman Mailer (*The Executioner's Song*)—despite advertisements for themselves—scarcely self-originate that, or true crime. The recursive novelization of true crime (again, taken as its own theme in Capote and Mailer) is a version of the media apriori in modern society (its emergence as a self-describing and self-observing system). The self-reflexive text repeats this insight—but as if foregrounding its self-observation and self-description were a way of getting back of it. The same goes for other versions of this "postmodern" turn: self-reflexivity is taken to mark a critical

postmodernism, as opposed to a conservative or affirmative one. (The distinction between critical and affirmative postmodernism—that is, between good and bad—proceeds as if a politics or an ethics were hardwired into objects. Hence the same artworks tend to show up on both sides of the divide—an embarrassment that leads to the discovery of ambivalence itself as the sign of the critical, if not of art itself.) To the extent that reflexivity is the social and philosophical condition and dilemma of modernity, it is not as if reflecting on it exempts oneself from it (nor does reflecting on that). The presumption continues that exposing social mechanisms undoes them. But the situation today is exactly the opposite: it is the exposure of these mechanisms that installs them, in that self-exposure is absolutely fundamental to their operation.

23. Ruth Rendell, *A Judgement in Stone* (New York: Vintage, 2000), 1.

24. L. H. Sigourney, *Letters of Life* (1867; New York, 1980), 39.

25. Catharine Maria Sedgwick, *Means and Ends, or Self-Training* (New York, 1842), 27.

26. William Dean Howells, *The Rise of Silas Lapham* (1885; New York: Norton, 1982), 104.

27. See chapter 5, "Vicarious Crime."

28. In Rendell's novel *A Demon in My View* (1976), this recirculation of Bartlett's and the literary cliché is itself literalized. The transparency of the media of communication in true and false crime is something more than generic self-consciousness. It is one measure of the manner in which the modern media survive their transparency and continue to function—or, rather, require that transparency in order to function. Put somewhat differently, if the media everywhere arises as its own subject in true crime and crime fiction, calling that "postmodern" does not take things very far. In fact, it points to the ways in which an attentiveness to medium specificity in a range of recent art theory and literary theory is often the sign of a remarkable inattentiveness to the specificity of the media in that theoretical work.

29. My concern here is not to survey the range of true or false crime but to indicate its media apriori and the style of reflexivity to which it acclimatizes readers and viewers. Consider, for a moment, another example, Eoin McNamee's extraordinary novel *The Blue Tango* (London: Faber and Faber, 2001). This novel too installs the *CSI* effect. It also imitates true crime in opening with a bare case summary that then gives way to its narration: "The narrator's voice falls away into conjecture. Her slaughter has been told but not the motive for it, and the face of her killer remains hidden. The narrator's voice falls away into hypothesis and surmise" (*Blue Tango*, p. ix). One difference here is that *The Blue Tango* does not, or does not merely,

imitate true crime in fictional form: it turns out to be a thorough investigation via novelization of a real-life case. The novel is thus a counterfactual forensic investigation. The mass media directly enter into the case and its prosecution—a real-life murder case that was on all counts bound up with media-sponsored life. (The cold case had, at the time of the novel's writing, recently resurfaced in the press after the long incarceration of the man convicted of the crime was overturned.) McNamee's fiction is then (like, it will be seen, Poe's "Mystery of Marie Roget") an attempt to solve a real crime: a real crime that (as with Poe) is bound up through and through, from motive to prosecution, with the media—and its mix of moral and feral intentions. But the registration of the media apriori goes beyond that: McNamee's novel is hyperliterary, often congealing in images and often taking on media dialects and ideolects. There is no indication within the text that the case is a real one (since any indication of that within the text would be self-disqualifying). Hence the novel inhabits the self-reflexive space of a media apriori that orchestrates its own dance (the blue tango).

30. Patricia Highsmith, *Those Who Walk Away* (New York: Atlantic Monthly Press, 1967), 57, 166.

31. On such bioscripts as part of the reflexive historicity of modernity, see Anthony Giddens, *Modernity and Self-Identity: Self and Society in the Late Modern Age* (Stanford, CA: Stanford University Press, 2001), especially chapter 3, "The Trajectory of the Self." For a somewhat "default" critique of this way of thinking about the modern subject and its psychology as a fall from real to popular psychology, see Slavoj Žižek, *The Ticklish Subject: An Essay in Political Ontology* (London: Verso, 1999), 341–347. My concern here is with the popularity of popular psychology and its media—with the paradox of psychic and social effects that survive their self-transparency and keep going anyway.

32. See Niklas Luhmann, "A Redescription of 'Romantic Art,'" *MLN: Modern Language Notes* 111, no. 3 (1996): 511; see also Luhmann, *The Reality of the Mass Media,* 114.

33. Erving Goffman, *Interaction Ritual: Essays on Face-to-Face Behavior* (New York: Pantheon, 1967), 262–263. I will be returning, in the final part of this study, to Goffman, among others, and to the cold war sociology of act and acting—in effect, to the sociology proper to the presentation of self in the everyday life of reality shows, candid cameras, vicarious life, and love and war games effected and exposed in the postwar mass media. The everyday life sociology of the fictionality that structures "real social situations" (Goffman, *The Presentation of Self in Everyday Life* [New York: Doubleday, 1959], 255) is, it will be seen, bound directly to the counterfactual realities

of the cold war and its media, its ways of thinking the unthinkable, modeling it, and playing it out.

34. Goffman, *Interaction Ritual,* 266.

35. That is, we are by now thoroughly familiar with the problems with "the risk
society": with the radical expansion of the scope and obligation to make
decisions along with the disbalancing of the grounds for making them (the
multiple choices of the risk society); with the promiscuous media construction and sampling of possible worlds (the information-saturated world that
thus compels and obviates making informed choices); with the compulsions of a decisionism that turns decision into something observed—without the capacity, or even the pressure, of deciding or acting.

36. See chapter 7, "Postscript on the Violence–Media Complex (and Other
Games)."

37. See Bernhard Siegert, *Relays: Literature as an Epoch of the Postal System,* trans.
Kevin Repp (Stanford, CA: Stanford University Press, 1999).

38. See my *Bodies and Machines* (New York: Routledge, 1992), particularly,
Part V, "The Love-Master." Here I would add that the prosthesis model is
itself part of the condition it diagnoses, in that it posits the human body
(and by extension personhood) as technology's axiom or point d'appui—
which is precisely what is in question.

39. That shift in attention from what a social system is to how it works may
seem a small one, but it is crucial in redescribing reflexive modernity and
its media infrastructure.

40. I mean to test out, that is, what it means to consider crime as a system and
a media form. Hence recent work in media theory (particularly the work
of Friedrich Kittler) and in system theory (particularly the work of Niklas
Luhmann) enter directly into the idiom and tendencies of the pages that
follow. It will become clear why the question as to whether these styles of
social and media analyses provide good accounts of the conditions of reflexive modernity or just good symptoms of them must itself remain unsettled.
For if (as Kittler puts it) "media determine our situation," and enter into our
thinking, they enter into our thinking about the media too. ("Media determine our situation, which—in spite or because of it—deserves a description." Friedrich A. Kittler, *Gramophone, Film, Typewriter,* trans. Geoffrey
Winthrop-Young and Michael Wutz [Stanford, CA: Stanford University
Press, 1999], xxxix). And if, as Luhmann puts it, "reflexivity may be the
predicament of the philosophy of this century," reflecting on that is part
of the same predicament. See Niklas Luhmann, "Deconstruction as Second-Order Observing," in *Theories of Distinction: Redescribing the Descriptions of Modernity,* ed. William Rasch (Stanford, CA: Stanford University,

2002), 112. But it is necessary at the same time to apply some pressure to these styles of description and analysis. A media determinism, or the media as social system, makes visible the same paradoxical logic we have been tracing. This is the case because the technological determination of forms of life would be at the same time the achievement of an absolute social self-determination. This paradox is one reason why American "new media" studies tend toward a ritually reasserted humanism (albeit often by way of a methodologically concealed conservatism). And it is one reason too why the rigorously unsentimentalized assertion of a media apriori (Kittler's, for example) registers but cannot account for the proliferation of violence and sexualized violence around new media formations (from serial violence to the military-entertainment complex). Nor does (Luhmann's) systems theory—cool in its allocation to persons of nothing but the position of "node of attribution"—have an interest in the proliferation of the violence that centers the mediatronic pathological public sphere.

41. Juan José Saer, *The Witness,* trans. Margaret Jull Costa (London: Serpent's Tail, 1990), 59. Hereafter abbreviated *Witness.*

42. Tzvetan Todorov, *The Conquest of America: The Question of the Other,* trans. Catherine Porter (Norman: Oklahoma University Press, 1999), 251. On the links between alphabetic writing and the praxis of reflexivity and critique, see also Marcel Detienne, *Les Savoirs de l'ecriture en Grece ancienne* (Lille: Du Septentrion, 1988).

43. It posits and includes therefore too its own state of exception, marking its self-distinction. The political notion of the state of exception is theorized by Carl Schmitt, specifically in relation to the discovery of America as the positing of Europe's state of exception (the New World as a sort of "violence brothel," a zone of legal and moral exemption). See Carl Schmitt, *Der Nomos der Erde im Völkerrecht des Jus Publicum Europaeum* (Berlin: Duncker & Humblot, 1988). Schmitt's notion of the state of exception has, more recently, been readapted and generalized in the work of Giorgio Agamben, as the contemporary state: "the political space of modernity" as the violence of the state of exception (with the death camp as its model) and the technological killing field as "the nomos of the modern." See Giorgio Agamben, *Homo Sacer: Sovereign Power and Bare Life,* trans. D. Heller-Roazen (Stanford, CA: Stanford University Press, 1988) and *State of Exception,* trans. Kevin Attell (Chicago: University of Chicago, 2005). Agamben's argument, historical only in the most messianic sense, registers modern life in terms of "the perfect senselessness to which the society of the spectacle condemns it" (*Homo Sacer,* 11). (For an astute account of Agamben in relation to Benjamin and Schmitt, see William Rasch, *Sovereignty and Its*

Discontents [London: Birkbeck Law Press, 2004]). And since it is scarcely necessary to make sense of the perfectly senseless, the "society of the spectacle" is occulted and media observation remains in effect unobserved, its violence generalized. The generalization of violence as the political space of modernity is the logic of a pathological public sphere, of a wound culture: a world of trauma and witnessing whose anthem is "everybody hurts" (REM) and whose slogan is "history is what hurts" (Fredric Jameson). (This is, as Jacques Rancière traces, part of the by now routine "transformations of avant-garde thinking into nostalgia" such that "the tradition of critical thinking has metamorphosed into deliberation on mourning." See *The Politics of Aesthetics*, trans. Gabriel Rockhill [London: Continuum, 2004], 9.) But the exact "fit" between the theoretical and popular self-description of the state of the modern may itself indicate the limits, the symptomatic character, of these descriptions and it may open the possibility of a redescription that does not await, as for Agamben (among others), the advent, indefinitely postponed, of a "completely new politics" (the "pure potentiality" of a "pure" law and language). At the least, Saer's story of media witnessing and the state of exception points to their mutual contingency and to the relays between modern violence and the media system, which is what concerns me here.

44. Corporate logo for Illusion, Inc. See chapter 7, "Postscript on the Violence–Media Complex (and Other Games)."

45. See chapter 5, "Vicarious Crime."

46. Elias Canetti, *Crowds and Power,* trans. Carol Stewart (New York: Noonday, 1984), 52.

47. See Giancarlo Corsi, "The Dark Side of a Career," in *Problems of Form,* ed. Dirk Baecker, trans. Michael Irmscher, with Leah Edwards (Stanford, CA: Stanford University Press, 1999), 243–244.

CHAPTER 2

The Conventions of True Crime

Crime and Commiseration

The style of public belief and popular memory called "reality TV" is one of the most conspicuous signs of the interactive compulsion in contemporary culture. And one of the most visible markers of reality TV—both in its true confession and its true crime formats—is the popularity of both stranger-intimacy and stranger-violence. The public spectacle of torn and private bodies and torn and private persons is also the spectacle of a style of sociality. That style of sociality has become inseparable from the mass exhibition and mass witnessing, the endlessly reproducible display, of wounded bodies and wounded minds in public—hence the trauma thing that has burgeoned in recent popular and academic culture; hence the lurid, albeit transient and quasi-anonymous, celebrity of the spokesvictims of what I have called our contemporary wound culture; hence too the manner in which crime, mass-mediated interiority, and publicness have been drawn into an absolute proximity in today's endless reality show.

The protocols of true crime are not hard to detect. The conventions of the genre are in fact instantly recognizable; in fact, there is nothing more recognizable about true crime than its utter conventionality. True crime is not just formulaic; it is a sort of writing or screening by numbers. And this hyperconventionality too is a crucial part of the story true crime tells.

Consider a recent case in point, a 1990s murder case that became something of a media sensation in the United States.

This case makes it possible to concisely locate some of the elementary particles of true crime.

Here is the lead "synopsis" of the case, provided by a Web site—one of Yahoo's top hundred sites, we are told—that has formed around the murder, its investigation, and (in signature true crime fashion) the investigation of the investigation:

The Robin Hood Hills Murders

May 5th, 1993 was a Wednesday, and when the Weaver Elementary School bell rang, three 8 year old boys headed home to their nearby West Memphis, Arkansas neighborhood. Only a few hours later they would be reported missing and an informal search by their parents would be under way.

The next afternoon at 1:45PM, a child's body was pulled from a creek in an area known as Robin Hood Hills. Eventually the bodies of the other two missing children were found nearby, and all three of them were naked and they had been tied ankle to wrist with their own shoe laces. The children had been severely beaten and one child, Christopher Byers, appears to have been the focus of the attack; he had been stabbed repeatedly in the groin area and castrated.

A triple homicide is extremely unusual, and particularly when the victims are children. The facts surrounding the case and the events which they triggered—the aftermath, the trials, the verdicts, and the hearings—have been the focus of an ongoing research project for the past several years.[1]

Three teenagers were arrested and convicted of the crime; one was sentenced to death. But the arrest and conviction have themselves seemed, at best, extremely unusual. It is this "aftermath" that has generated the ongoing "research project": a project that amounts to a sort of Internet-centered criminal justice cottage industry. That industry centers on the missing truth of the crime. For one thing, the evidence against the alleged killers appears slight, dubious, and unconvincing. For another, rumors of satanic rituals—the perfunctory paraphernalia of a satanic panic—surrounded the case and made their way into the prosecution, as did a range of what might be called lifestyle evidence: black-dressing, goth style; enthusiasm for heavy-metal music; and, in the case of the prosecution's central target, a teenager who (unfortunately) had adopted the horror-genre–associated name of Damien, sporadic interest in earth religions, versions of white witchcraft, and so forth.

This is what a quick synopsis of the case—media-named the West Memphis 3—looks like. But it may already be clear that the popularity of the case centers on something else. The media circuit justice—the so-called "research projects" and proliferating support groups that have grown up around the case—centers not on the murders themselves or quite on the murder investigation or trial. It centers on the prosecution of the prosecution; that is, it centers on the ongoingness of the "ongoing research project" itself.

True crime is a way of returning to the scene of the crime by way of its recreation and representation. True crime always involves an aesthetics of the aftermath: a forensic realism.[2] The forensic way of seeing is held steadily visible here, for instance, in the deadpan and dispassionate description of graphic horrors in the case summary. But graphic horror quickly yields to research, bodies yield to information. The forensic procedures of true crime are inseparable from the self-reflexiveness of the communicative media of contemporary information culture; information culture endlessly reports on itself, as the media always interviews itself about itself. The mistake would be to reduce this reflexivity to a species of self-consciousness; it is instead reflexive modernity's style of sociality—sociality in scare quotes.

True crime, along these lines, loops back on itself; the radical entanglement of crime, information, and spectacle is everywhere in evidence here. More exactly, the spectacle of the torn and open body is also the conversion of bodies into information. And the conversion of bodies into information is also the opening of the torn and private body, the torn and private person, to public spectacle. The term *forensics*, it will be recalled, derives from "forum" or publicness. In a wound culture, it is precisely the spectacle of the torn and private body that becomes the gathering point of the public as such. On the autopsy table, pornography and forensics meet and fuse. In wound culture, the mass spectacle of the torn and opened body is the relay point of private fantasy and public space.[3]

But what one discovers in true crime, in forensic realism more generally, is not merely the conversion of bodies into information and information into spectacle. Something new and something strange is at work here. What one discovers in true crime is the entering of the mass spectacle into the interior of modern violence; crime, bodies, and spectacle refer back to each other at every point. What this looks like will take some unpacking. Hence, I want to take up, in preliminary fashion and initially by way of the case of the West Memphis 3, three constituent elements of true crime: first, the relation of fact and fiction in true crime; second, true crime's way of mapping public space; and, third, the relays between the scene of the crime and the scene of publicness itself. It will then be possible to thicken this description of true crime and to indicate some of its larger cultural implications.

First, the fact/fiction thing. No doubt true crime puts in doubt from the start the line between fact and fiction. The very notion of true crime, I have suggested, proceeds as if "crime" itself were assumed to be a fictional thing, such that the word "true" must be added to bend it toward fact; the line between crime fact and crime fiction is in play from the start. I am referring not merely to the fact that, for instance, the Federal Bureau of Investigation (FBI) profilers, in their training courses, read the early crime fictions of Poe along with the recent ones of pulp novelists such as Thomas Harris. Poe plagiarized the "true" crime press in renovating crime detection fiction. Harris plagiarizes true crime writing too—not least the self-fictionalizations of the FBI profilers themselves. The looping effect, or unremitting reflexivity, always at work here could not be clearer. Hence there are the profilers' own contributions to a sort of gothic subgenre of true crime: true crime bestsellers with titles such as *Whoever Fights Monsters* and *Journey into Darkness*. As one profiler (a cofounder of the FBI's Behavioral Sciences Unit) straightforwardly put it, "Our antecedents actually do go back to crime fiction more than crime fact."[4]

What exactly does this coming down of the boundaries between fact and fiction in these cases mean? True crime operates in that counterfactual region between truth and falsity: the region of social and collective belief, the situation of modern credibility. But if in true crime the boundary line between fact and fiction comes down, this means something more. That is because what that line between fiction (fantasy) and fact (public reality) polices is also something like the boundary line between private desire and public space. True crime has become something like a cultural flashpoint, a strange attractor, on the contemporary American scene, and part of its attraction is this: the testing of the public/private divide, in all its normalcy and in all its incoherence, a retesting of the gap between private fantasy and public reality in contemporary culture.

A brief return to the West Memphis 3 case can make this nexus of truth and publicness a bit clearer. I have briefly set out a synopsis of the case, relying in part on the "new to the site: read this first" synopsis provided on the wm3.org Web site. But the synopsis is a bit misleading. What triggered the project and what has generated the astonishing burgeoning of support groups around this case is, in fact, a film—an HBO documentary called, somewhat uncertainly, *Paradise Lost: The Robin Hood Hills Murders*. This indecisively factual film, we are told on the Internet, has "with a little help from the Internet," created an avalanche of support for the three convicted killers.

The film, which is intent on exposing the prosecution as a witch-hunt, is the primary database for these support groups. One discovers again and again, in scanning the statements of the virtual support groups, testimony on the part of supporters or fans of the case, an initial uncertainty about whether the film was fact or fiction. After all, a fictional-documentary effect has, for some time, been adapted to the genre of the murder film (for example, the extraordinary pseudodocumentary, the Belgian film *Man Bites Dog*, or, more recently, the Poe-like documentary hoax, *The Blair Witch Project*). Films such as these do not merely simulate documentary and the documentary representation of violence. These films foreground the ways in which modern violence has become inseparable from the mass-mediated relaying of violence. Modern violence makes visible the strange and unprecedented *intimacy* of modern technologies of representation and reproduction, copying and transmission. The reality of the mass media is installed rather than vitiated by the exposure of its special effects; the reality of the mass media is a self-installing and thus self-exposing reality. Hence, it is scarcely surprising that the same team that has coordinated the paralegal project *Paradise Lost* recently entered into another film venture—the making of another documentary of sorts, the sequel to *The Blair Witch Project*. Nor should it be surprising that *Book of Shadows: Blair Witch 2*—which calls itself "a fictional reenactment of real events"—draws directly on the facts of the West Memphis 3 case.

The popular criminology of reality TV, and the documentaries that look like it, make visible the structure of what counts as public today: "events and issues only become *public* in the full sense when the means exist whereby the separate worlds of professional and lay person, of controller and controlled, are brought into relation with one another and appear, for a time at least, to occupy the same space."[5] The interactive compulsion that drives, for instance, reality TV shows such as *America's Most Wanted*—where the audience participates in lay policing or vigilantism, tracking down criminals—is just such a mingling of the worlds of the professional and the lay person, the relay point of a sort of phantasmatic expertness and viewers like you and me. (Or, as Hannibal Lecter, the consummate professional as psycho killer, puts it in the recent film *Hannibal:* "*Lay person,* interesting term.")

What that compulsion constructs is then not merely public space but public space as the interactive scene of the crime. And this generalization of the scene of the crime such that the national scene and the crime scene become two ways of saying the same thing is one version of what I have elsewhere described as the emergence of a pathological public sphere. Here the home world incipiently becomes its own state of exception: that is, that world becomes its own violence brothel. But that world then, like that of the graphic-novel-turned-film *Sin City,* is one that, visibilizing its media, is a doubly observed world—and therefore a half-believed one.

The Violence–Normality Paradox

What, then, does public space—the pathological public sphere—in true crime look like? And how does it relate to what I have called the hyperconventionality of the genre? For the moment, I want to touch on what might be called the normal scene of true crime—that is, what true crime takes as normal—or, more exactly, abnormally normal. The temporary disruption of the normal public order and its recovery is perhaps the by-now default way of understanding the procedure and appeal of the "classic" detective story and the classic crime drama. But contemporary true crime has somewhat different premises.

The normal in the world of true crime is always a bit too normal, abnormally normal. In part, the West Memphis native informants of the documentary *Paradise Lost* resemble the wound culture underclass of reality TV crime shows such as *Cops,* a population on exhibition that has slipped through the cracks of American normalcy.[6] These are not the mediagenic spokesmodels of American normality (not, say, the endlessly permutable cast of *Friends*). They are something like the opposite, living outside the precincts of the national reality show. The population of reality TV crime shows or *Paradise Lost* images a world of physical overembodiment and fundamentalist overbelief; the inhabitants recite the clichés and wear the styles of a national normality but do not inhabit them. Put simply, they exhibit the opposite of the sort of exhibition of an ideal-typical normality that Douglas Coupland neatly captures in his recent novel *Miss Wyoming:* a model American home "whose normalcy was so extreme she felt she had magically leapt five hundred years into the future and was inside a diorama recreating middle-class North American life in the late twentieth century."[7] Normality takes the form of a theme-park replica of itself, referring to an elsewhere that inhabits and scripts the everyday. Here is Coupland again: "'How do you want us to act, Mr. Johnson?' 'Oh Jesus. How about *normal.*' This remark drew a blank. 'Normal?' Cindy asked. 'Like housewives? Like people who live in Ohio or something?'" (*Miss Wyoming,* p. 45).

Consider, again, the synopsis of the Robin Hood Hills murder case, "May 5th, 1993 was a Wednesday," and so on. The conventions of true crime's forensic realism are immediately visible. That realism involves the sudden eruption of violence from beneath a therefore deceptively normal surface of things; that is, it involves the convention of penetrating beneath convention, beneath the clichés, of an everyday and statistical normality (a Wednesday, a school day, a neighborhood, a family). This is, more precisely, the stripping away of a *fiction* of normality—the normal fiction:

a normality that looks like nothing but a self-exposing childhood fantasy of innocence, a Robin Hood story, a paradise lost. The convention of innocence yields quickly and conventionally to a gothicized horror, and true crime is a modern variant of that cliché machine called the gothic.

In this first documentary on the case, there is the story of the happy family and idyllic boyhood violated. There is also a second HBO documentary, *Revelations: Paradise Lost Revisited.* The sequel shifts the focus, making its case for the guilt of the father of the most brutally attacked and tortured of the three little boys. Hence, the story of the happy family satanically invaded from without (Save the Family!) turns round to the story of a demonic intrafamilial violence (Save Us from the Family!). The story of boyhood innocence murdered (Save the Children!) turns round to a story of murderous boys (Save Us from the Children!). And, of course, these opposed but coupled stories have structured the popular psychology of an unrepentant and hothouse familialism on the American scene, its minglings of murder and intimacy, from later eighteenth-century true crime to the present.[8]

Here one discovers what might be called the violence–normality paradox. Take, for instance, the recent Arnold Schwarzenegger film *The Sixth Day.* The "sixth day" refers to the sixth day of creation, the making of man and woman, and the film centers on "sixth day" laws—laws against the threat to natural persons and the natural family posed by the unnatural making of cloning. But in this context, the opening sequence of the film poses some problems. The opening sequence exploits, as it were, the automaton-like acting of the central actor. It constructs an utterly artificial situation-comedy family—ideal-typical wife-mother, husband-father, daughter, family pet—and these ideal-typical persons recite to each other the clichés of the mass-mediated, mass-produced American family. That is to say, the exotic threat of cloning persons and families registers exactly in reverse the real threat, the recognition that persons and families are already clones. That threat—an effect of doubling via the technical media—can then be reinvisibilized by way of the futurist threat of technical doubling (cloning). The unnaturalness of the natural family, its abnormal normality, is precisely then the paramnesic symptom of the film: what it images and what it disavows. Beyond that, the media determination of our situation becomes its own symptom too.

"Normal Americans," it has recently been argued, "are driven by the desire to be normal."[9] Normal Americans, that is, are driven by the desire to be as normal as everyone else. This is the backside of the democratic idea: the extreme ramification of equality such that one yields to an identification with an indeterminate number of others. This is the numerical or statistical normality of statistical persons. And this is, of course, simply the refrain of a pathological conformity tracked from Tocqueville to the invasion-of-the-body-snatchers "clone" panic (the organization man, our uneasy little man in the gray-flannel suit, the adjusted American, the other-directed American) that became sociology and popular sociology in the 1950s and 1960s.

Consider, for example, Snell and Gail J. Putney's 1964 study, *The Adjusted American: Normal Neuroses in the Individual and Society*. The study begins by reciting an account of the underside of the democratic idea:

> "When I survey this countless multitude of beings, shaped to each other's likeness ... the sight of such universal uniformity saddens and chills me, and I am tempted to regret that state of society which has ceased to be ... every citizen, being assimilated to all the rest, is lost in the crowd." Familiar words! But they were not written by David Riesman, not even in the twentieth century. They were written by Comte Alexis de Tocqueville ... in 1831.[10]

That is, by 1964 the analysis of conformity was already a self-instancing one; it already had the status of a national cliché. After all, we read that "Moreover, for a decade or more, social critics from David Riesman to Vance Packard to the Sunday supplement writers have presented to an ever-widening audience a portrait of the American as an 'other-directed,' status seeking conformist."[11] The very nondistinction between academic and paperback sociology—that is, the very popularity of popular sociology—thus becomes in effect the index of conformity: "Riesman coined the phrase 'other-direction' and struck a responsive chord with Americans. They seized on the phrase, for it seemed to name and to delineate something in their fellows—and in themselves."[12] For this reason, the central claim is that "the startling change in conformity in thus not in the degree of conformity, but in the general *consciousness* of conformity."[13] At the same time, however, the antidote to conformity—the breakthrough to autonomy—is seen in this way: "The prerequisite to such a breakthrough is to become fully conscious of those beliefs [for example, conformity] which are so familiar that they are seldom remarked."[14] But since the general consciousness of conformity, and its endless remarking, from expert-professional sociology to the Sunday supplements, is the very premise of the study, this prerequisite stalls in incoherence.

More exactly, it makes visible the premises of a popular psychology and a popular sociology, that collective spectacle of the emotional tie or the social tie reflecting back on itself. It makes visible too something more: a resistless and self-transparent conformity to social norms without belief in them, the popularity of a popular psychology and a popular sociology not at all vitiated by the exposing of its mechanisms (just as the contemporary subgenre "the making of *X*" secures a fiction seen through from both sides).

The desire to be normal thus marks the entry into a closed loop of normalization; one desires to become the norm that one is, to cite the public opinions and beliefs that one, as one of any number of others, has. Hence public culture "needs only, by means of opinion polls and statistics, to proliferate its citation of those phantom witnesses"—and these phantom witnesses, who believe in our place, "articulate our existences by teaching us what they should be."[15] In effect, one believes through the other without exactly believing oneself: "belief thus functions on the basis of the value of the real that is assumed 'anyway' in the other, even when one knows perfectly well—all too well—the extent to which 'it's all bullshit' on one's own side."[16] This is the condition of referred belief that true crime, in its mass-media mingling of violence and normality, posits as publicness.

The National Conversation

Put simply, true crime, like pulp fiction, is made up of clichés. It is, more precisely, about clichés in that clichés are about publicness. The mistake is to reduce the cliché to mere cliché, in that the cliché voices popular psychology and popular sociology and does so with the self-evidence of the weather. It reflects the social tie back to itself (intimating that it consists in that and nothing but that; see Chapter 5, "Vicarious Crime").

Here we might instance the practice of one of the best-selling American true crime writers, Ann Rule. In a press release accompanying a recent book, *Bitter Harvest* (about family violence in the American "heartland"), Rule sets out the formula that governs the cases she covers. "It has to have an [antihero] who has at least some of the following characteristics: charisma, intelligence, education, wealth, beauty, fame—all the things most people think would make them happy. ... They seem to be perfect."[17] Her case studies have names such as "You Belong to Me," "Black Christmas," "One Trick Pony," "Everything She Ever Wanted," and so forth. Her accounts open like this: "Charles and Annie Goldmark and their sons ... seemed the least likely family to encounter a killer. ... He was brilliant, thoughtful, and kind. Annie ... was a lovely woman at forty-three. She was sparkling and vivacious. ... The Goldmarks epitomized what was good about the American family."[18] Or, again: "When lovely, blond Vonnie Stuth and her husband were married on May 4, 1974, the future looked as bright as a Northwest sunrise. And well it should have. They were very much in love, he had a good job, and Vonnie planned to work as a volunteer case aide."[19] Or, yet again: "On July 9, 1979, Stacy Sparks's life was not only completely normal, it was filled with happy plans."[20]

True crime reads like bad fiction (false crime), and not simply in that if it read like good fiction it would interfere with its claims to truth. True crime cannot cease referring to the fictionality that would seem to intercept its truth. True crime, that is, cannot cease referring to the clichés of national normality even as it intercepts their credibility. Put somewhat differently, true crime cannot cease referring to the mass-mediated and technical conditions of intimacy and relation—the protocols of interiority and sociality—that then are seen to void intimacy and relation.

In short, true crime is about what truth looks like, what belief looks like, and what relation—intimate and collective—looks like in a mass-public wound culture: this is at once its banality and its popularity. True crime does so most economically in its unremitting delegation of truth, normality, and relation to the idiom of mass credibility, to the popular psychology and popular sociology of the cliché.

Consider the prototypical or statistical person, one of the superstars of America's wound culture, a "type of nonperson" in whom sheer violence and sheer typicality indicate each other at every point. That is, the murderer by numbers called the serial killer. There are a range of popular misconceptions about this type of person (and I have traced these misconceptions elsewhere). But for the moment, I am interested precisely in what makes these misconceptions, and hence this type of person, popular and compelling.

The composite serial killer always looks like a composite, the statistical picture of a kind of person. Serial killing is also called stranger-killing. The serial killer is always "the stranger beside me" or "everyone's next-door neighbor": "average-looking" and "just like yourself." As Jim Thompson puts it in his generically titled novel *The Criminal,* he is above all generic: "How many of these sex murderers are ever run down? You can't type them on modus operandi; they're not peculiar to any particular group or class. They look like you and me and everyone else, and they *are* you and me and everyone else."[21] The stranger in the lonely crowd is one who is near but also far; he is abnormally normal, the violence–normality paradox in person.

The Stranger beside Me is the title of Ann Rule's true crime story of the serial killer Ted Bundy. Bundy, while a student at the University of Washington—majoring in abnormal psychology, of course—had a work–study job at a suicide prevention and crisis hotline. One of his volunteer coworkers and friends at the hotline was the young true crime writer Rule, a contributor to *True Detective* magazine who had contracted to write a book on the recent "Ted" killings in the Seattle area (that is, on her friend Bundy himself). Not surprisingly, Rule's book wavers between shock (he could not have done it, I *know* him) and journalistic happiness (after all, what luck!). Her book insistently tells two stories at once: a story about murder and a story about writing—such that the media apriori is installed in true crime's own crisis hotline.

True crime writing and its twin pulp fiction are the genre fictions of the body proper to a wound culture. Pulp fiction, like true crime, is premised precisely on the direct communication between two senses of pulp:

as mass-produced representations and as massy bodily and psychic interiors. It is about the experience of torn bodies and torn persons inseparable from an intimation of the mass-mediation of bodies and persons. The coupling of mass-mediated clichés and graphic violence that governs such writing is also a coupling of violence and an experience or intimation of being formed from the outside in. That is, put most simply, the experience of relation—sexual or collective—as mass-mediation and of mass-mediation as violation and as wounding.[22]

This is nowhere clearer than in the type of person who is also something like the mass in person called the serial killer. Bundy, for example, struck everyone as perfectly chameleon-like: just similar. It was observed again and again that "he never looked the same from photograph to photograph." Bundy's death row interviews are endless strings of mass-media and pop-academic clichés. The interviews read as if the pages of *Psychology Today* directed his words, his eyes, his face, his mind. They are spoken in the third person, where he lived.

Along the same lines, the pages of true crime and of pulp fiction perfect the voice-over of an indirect discourse, a yielding of first person to third person, in the mass idiom and medium of the personalized cliché. Or as Bundy, a type of nonperson who also described himself as "a very verbal person," expressed it, "Personalized stationery is one of the small but truly necessary luxuries of life."[23]

Here are samples of Bundy's way of speaking about what he called "socializing type"—that is, personal—relations. He described his mother in his quasi-personalized confessions entirely in terms of her relation to words and writing: "My mother taught me the English language. ... How many times did she type my papers as I dictated them to her? [She] gave me great verbal skills. ... I could have written them out in shorthand but would dictate things I had left out." His mother, he continued, has "beautiful handwriting, very good vocabulary, but she never *says* anything! She says, 'I love you,' or 'I'm sorry we haven't written. Everything's fine," or 'We miss you. ... Everything will turn out.' ... 'Blah, blah, blah.'"[24]

In short, persons for Bundy were faceless numbers and types in a media loop: "I mean, there are *so* many people. ... Terrible with names ... *and* faces. Can't remember faces."[25] That is, persons, faces, and names, for this very verbal person, are a defaced and dead language, the dead repetitions that register intimacy ("I love you") only as a worn quotation, a dictated, typed, stereotyped interiority. Writing, dictation, typing, shorthand, communication technologies, the data stream, pulp fiction and the true crime genre, the mass media and mediatronic intimacy—all traverse these cases, enter into the interior of this style of "unmotivated" violence, a violence seen as unmotivated, impersonal, compulsive, and as collectively intimate, as the cliché.

This kind of crime and this kind of person have their places in a public culture in which addictive violence has become not merely a collective spectacle but also one of the crucial sites where private desire and public space cross.[26] The convening of the public around scenes of mass-mediated violence has come to make up a wound culture: the public fascination with torn and open bodies and torn and opened psyches, a public gathering around shock, trauma, and the wound.

One of the preconditions of our contemporary wound culture is the emergence of popular genres of collective intimacy, such as, for example, the popularity of true crime (and the forensic apriori and the trauma apriori) that make up the two dominant forms of reality TV. (See also Chapter 6, "Berlin 2000.") And one of the general preconditions of the contemporary pathological public sphere is the emergence of psychology as public culture: the opening to view, the mass observation, of each and every body and psyche.

Stranger-intimacy is bound up not merely with the conditions of urban proximity in anonymity (one of the preconditions of modern crime) but also with its counterpart: the emergence of intimacy in public. The romance of American psychology corresponds roughly to the post–World War II era: the period in which subjectivity and its management was renovated as growth industry: the industry of growing persons in both expert professional and popular culture. As C. Wright Mills observed in 1951, "We need to characterize American society of the mid-twentieth century in more psychological terms, for now the problems that concern us most border on the psychiatric."[27]

The bordering of the social on the psychiatric becomes visible on several fronts in the postwar decades: in the spreading of the mental health profession and in the abnormal normality of psychic pain ("psychological help was defined so broadly that everyone needed it"); in the transformation of patient into "client" and "mental health" into something that could be mass produced and purchased; in the rise of sociologistic psychologies of self-actualization (the work of Carl Rogers and Abraham Maslow, among others); and in the proliferation of psychologistic sociologies of collective and national psychopathology (from the inaugural diagnosis of "American nervousness" to future shock and the culture of narcissism to Prozac nation and the trauma culture of the 1990s). There appears an insatiable public demand—in the print media, drama, films, and television—for accessible, entertaining, interactive information on psychological disturbances and psy-experts: "private ordeals" become "a matter of great public curiosity and untiring investigation."[28]

Stranger-intimacy and its maladies become public culture, part of a pathological public sphere. Take, for example, the talking cure as mass-media event: talk radio. It has been observed that there is a certain "paradox of radio: a universally public transmission is heard in the most private of circumstances."[29] One might easily reverse the terms of this paradox: the paradox of talk radio is that a private communication is heard in the most public of circumstances. The boundaries between public and private come down, in the collective gathering round private ordeals. The serial killer Ted Bundy described himself as a "radio freak" who "in my younger years ... depended a lot on the radio."[30] From about the sixth grade on, one of his favorite programs was a San Francisco radio talk show:

> I'd really get into it. It was a call-in show ... I'd listen to talk shows all day. ... I genuinely derived pleasure from listening to people talk at that age. It gave me comfort ... a lot of the affection I had for programs of that type came not because of their content, but because it was people talking! And I was eavesdropping on their conversations.[31]

The conversation has become an observer event (as in, for example, the media-sponsored life of a film like *The Conversation*).

And this version of the interactive compulsion was taken a step further in the psychology student's work–study job at the crisis hotline. As

Bundy's true crime biographer Ann Rule recounts, "The two of us were all alone in the building, connected to the outside world only by the phone lines. ... We were locked in a boiler room of other people's crises ... constantly talking to people about their most intimate problems."[32]

The true crime writer never strays far from the popularity of popular psychology: the abnormal normality of these stranger-intimacies and the mass observation of them. And precisely for that reason—for the reason that the social borders on the psychiatric in wound culture—the true crime writer maps social and national space by way of psychopathology. Rule, for example, alternates the openings of her formula case histories, shifting between stereotypical persons and stereotypical scenes—between popular psychology and popular sociology. Here is one opening scene:

> The I-95 Interstate snakes all along the eastern seaboard of the United States, beginning on the border between Maine and New Brunswick, Canada, and ending in Miami. Some who have reason to know say that parts of 95 are the most dangerous stretches of road in America. It is certainly one of the busiest freeways and one of the first ever laid down across the land. Down and down 95 plunges. ... Families travel I-95 as they head for Disney World.[33]

And so on. Here is another: "The state of Washington is cut in half by the Cascade Mountains ... Ellensburg and Yakima are in the middle of orchard country. ... You put an apple or cherry twig in irrigated land there and it will take root overnight. Or so it seems."[34]

These landscapes are psychotopographies, incipient crime scenes. It is not merely that social space is pathologized as the generalized scene of the crime. The tie between psychic and social life—the social tie—is here nothing but the psychotechnologies of everyday life (for example, the technical motion industries, automobiles and movies). Nor is it merely ("Or so it seems") that this gothicization of Disney America, in the very obtrusiveness of its gothic clichés (snakes in a theme park Eden), can scarcely be experienced as convincing. The violence–normality paradox is literally mapped onto public space. But the overexplicitness of such themes—their overt appearance as theme-park replicas of normality—is precisely the point. It is not just that such clichés are experienced as unconvincing, half-voided of belief and conviction. This lack of conviction in no way mitigates the force of such referred speech. For the "common experience of a degree of fictitiousness" is exactly the measure of popular belief today, the delegated or interactive condition of belief today.[35] The point not to be missed is that commonplaces are also common places. The shared or referred experience of such clichés as unconvincing is the condition of their popularity and force.

Crime and Togetherness

For the moment it is possible less to explain than to exemplify these conditions of referred experience and belief across the fact/fiction divide. Let me first set out one final and typical instance of true crime and its scenes. Here is the opening of *Wasteland* by the veteran true crime writer Michael Newton. The book tells the story of Charles Starkweather, the 1950s spree-killer on whom the Terence Malick film *Badlands* was based.

The 1950s

> Looking back through the distorting lens of memory, it seems to be a golden time. Prosperity. The baby boom. Tract homes and stylish cars. Walt Disney. ... A little help from Hollywood transforms the postwar decade into *Happy Days*. ...
>
> Like most myths, the illusion of the Fabulous Fifties has a kernel of truth. You didn't have to live in California to enjoy the sights of Disneyland, once television took the place of radio in American homes. ... *McCall's* magazine introduced "togetherness," a concept so popular that it took on the aspect of a social crusade and became the next best thing to a national purpose in the 1950s.[36]

The history of the 1950s is itself presented as a fantasy world. But it is not exactly that public fantasy is stripped away in this account. Instead, public fantasy—a phantasmatic normality—is its "kernel of truth." This is the logic of true crime—true crime as the terrain of true lies. The crime scene here is nothing but the nation scene. And if the popular media made popular the notion of "togetherness," this means that what binds the nation together is nothing deeper than the popular sociology of the social bond.

This is the self-reflexivity of mass public culture at its purest. And this self-reflexivity enters directly into Starkweather's motives and style of violence. For one thing, Starkweather identified without reserve with the celebrity icons of the 1950s, icons who conformed to the popular myth of nonconformity. Hence Starkweather imitated the icon who has been called America's first teenager, James Dean. And Dean, in turn, imitated celebrity rebels without a cause (sometimes signing his letters "James-Brando-Clift-Dean"). Starkweather, who saw himself as "everybody's nobody,"[37] was a sort of imitation machine. Attempting to achieve celebrity through his writings after his arrest, he wrote what Newton describes as "wild flights of melodrama strung together with clichés, sprawling over two hundred pages."[38]

But this is nothing but the idiom of true crime itself. Hence, Newton typically describes scenes in this way: "Bob showed up in his letterman's jacket, looking for all the world like an extra from *Happy Days*. They were the all-American couple, blissfully unaware of their impending rendezvous with Death."[39] Hence this description of Starkweather's partner in crime, Caril Ann Fugate, a description that falls back on clichés at the same time as it exposes just that:

> Authors searching for descriptions of Caril Ann after the fact, inevitably fall back on cliches about how absolutely *normal* she appeared. One found her "a typical, colorless, teenaged girl in a normal, nondramatic, midwestern setting," while another pegged her as "a perfect assimilation of the attitudes, fads, and fashions of the times." And both are correct. ... The trouble, typically, began at home.[40]

Quotation is (as Certeau indicates) the ultimate weapon for making one believe: that is, it is a technology for generating belief through the other. But quotation and the cliché—the quotation of no one in particular—

here work a bit differently. The self-reflexivity of true crime is the opposite of a critical distance; it is perfectly compatible with a suspended belief in what it at the same time affirms. The crucial point is this: this style of reflexivity realizes to the letter the paradox of a conformity with social norms without direct belief in them. It takes part in the circulation of convictions experienced as unconvincing, except to others like oneself. The mistake is to understand this paradoxicality as *undoing* this state of belief; it is, rather, its mode of operation.

This is the style of belief that inheres in the pathological public sphere. In the 1950s popular media advanced the notion of "togetherness"—a social crusade of sociality. In the 1990s togetherness mutated into something else: what might be called the sociality of the wound, a togetherness that takes the form of commiseration. The support groups that proliferate around the case of the West Memphis 3 instance just this: a public gathering into a public around the scene of the crime, the emergence of the public as support group, grouping in commiseration.

What has emerged on the contemporary scene is a style of sociality in the media spectacle of crime, violation, and shared (or referred) victimhood. But what has emerged too is a sense of the fictionality of this social bond. Hence it may be appropriate to end with three rapid examples of how contemporary fiction itself makes sense of commiseration and its public.

In his recent novel *Cocaine Nights,* J. G. Ballard posits crime as the gathering point of the contemporary public:

> But how do you energize people, give them some sense of community? ... Only one thing is left which can rouse people, threaten them directly and force them to act together. ... Crime, and transgressive behavior. ... Here transgressive behaviour is for the public good.[41]

But at the same time, this very theory of crime and publicness is disbelieved, reduced to nothing but what Ballard calls "paperback sociology."

Chuck Palahniuk's recent novel *Fight Club* migrates from the commiseration of support clubs to the formation of national community in

spectacles of pain and bodily violence—the "fight clubs," which are themselves "Support groups. Sort of."[42] Large questions of social and individual
identity are posed. As one of his characters puts it, "Maybe self-improvement isn't the answer. ... Maybe self-destruction is the answer" (p. 49).
But at the same time, these large questions appear as hollow ones. The
binding of self-realization and self-destruction appears as nothing but the
tokens of a voided self-reflexivity: "Why did I cause so much pain? Didn't
I realize that each of us is a sacred, unique snowflake of special unique
specialness (p. 207)?"

The main character of Michel Houellebecq's recent novel *Whatever*
experiences his abnormal normality to the letter: he calls himself "a fitting
symbol of this vital exhaustion. No sex drive, no ambition; no real interests either ... I consider myself a normal kind of guy. Well, perhaps not
completely normal, but who is completely, huh? Eighty percent normal,
let's say."[43] At one point in the novel, he hurls an object at a mirror and
dutifully reports this self-reflexive moment to his psychiatrist: "I raised my
eyes, looked her way. She had a somewhat astonished air. Finally she came
out with: 'That's interesting, the mirror. ...' She must have read something
in Freud, or in the *Mickey Mouse Annual*" (*Whatever,* pp. 146–147). Paperback sociology and Mickey Mouse psychology: "whatever" is perhaps by
now something like the technical term for the technologies of belief, commiseration, and publicness I have been sketching out here and want to fill
in, in the pages that follow.

Notes

1. Burk Sauls, "Synopsis of the Case," *Free the West Memphis 3*, http://
   www.wm3.org.
2. Ralph Rugoff, ed., *Scene of the Crime* (Cambridge, MA: MIT Press, 1997),
   18–20.
3. Mark Seltzer, *Serial Killers: Death and Life in America's Wound Culture*
   (New York: Routledge, 1998), 2–24.
4. John Douglas and Mark Olshaker, *Mindhunter: Inside the FBI's Elite Serial
   Crime Unit* (New York: Scribner, 1995), 95, 32.
5. Stuart Hall et al., *Policing the Crisis: Mugging, the State and Law and Order*
   (London: Macmillan, 1978), 145.

6. Elayne Rapping, "Aliens, Nomads, Mad Dogs, and Road Warriors: Tabloid TV and the New Face of Criminal Violence," in *Mythologies of Violence in Postmodern Media,* ed. Christopher Sharrett (Detroit, MI: Wayne State University Press, 1999), 249–273.

7. Douglas Coupland, *Miss Wyoming* (London: Flamingo, 2000), 19.

8. See David Brion Davis, *Homicide in American Fiction, 1798–1860* (Ithaca, NY: Cornell University Press, 1957); Karen Halttunen, *Murder Most Foul: The Killer and the American Gothic Imagination* (Cambridge, MA: Harvard University Press, 1998).

9. Mary Poovey, "Sex in America," *Critical Inquiry* 24, no. 2 (Winter 1998): 372.

10. Snell Putney and Gail J. Putney, *The Adjusted American: Normal Neuroses in the Individual and Society* (New York: Harper & Row, 1964), 1.

11. Putney and Putney, *The Adjusted American,* 3.

12. Putney and Putney, *The Adjusted American,* 71.

13. Putney and Putney, *The Adjusted American,* 2

14. Putney and Putney, *The Adjusted American,* 7.

15. Michel de Certeau, "Believing and Making People Believe," in *The Certeau Reader,* ed. Graham Ward (Oxford: Blackwell, 2000), 119–126.

16. Certeau, "Believing," 126–128.

17. Ann Rule, *Bitter Harvest* (New York: Simon & Schuster, 1997) (press release).

18. Ann Rule, "Black Christmas," in *You Belong to Me and Other True Cases* (New York: Warner Books, 1994), 281.

19. Ann Rule, "The Computer Error and the Killer," in *You Belong to Me,* 371.

20. Ann Rule, "The Vanishing," in *You Belong to Me,* 399.

21. Jim Thompson, *The Criminal* (1953; New York: Vintage, 1993), 88.

22. On Bundy, see Seltzer, *Serial Killers,* 5–12.

23. Bundy, quoted by Ann Rule, *The Stranger beside Me* (New York: Signet, 1989), 221.

24. Stephen G. Michaud and Hugh Aynesworth, *Ted Bundy: Conversations with a Killer* (New York: Signet, 1989), 10.

25. Bundy, quoted in Michaud and Aynesworth, *Ted Bundy,* 104.

26. See Seltzer, *Serial Killers.*

27. C. Wright Mills, *White Collar: The American Middle Classes* (New York: Oxford University Press, 1951), 160.

28. Ellen Herman, *The Romance of American Psychology: Political Culture in the Age of Experts* (Berkeley: University of California Press, 1995), 12-15, 262, 311, et passim.

29. Alan S. Weiss, *Phantasmic Radio* (Durham: Duke University Press, 1995), 6.

30. Michaud and Aynesworth, *Ted Bundy,* 7.

31. Michaud and Aynesworth, *Ted Bundy,* 10–11.

32. Ann Rule, *The Stranger beside Me*, 25.

33. Ann Rule, *You Belong to Me*, 5.

34. Ann Rule, *You Belong to Me,* 333.

35. Margaret Morse, *Virtualities: Television, Media Art, and Cyberculture* (Bloomington: Indiana University Press, 1998), 103.

36. Michael Newton, *Wasteland: The Savage Odyssey of Charles Starkweather and Carol Ann Fugate* (New York: Pocket, 1998), 1–3.

37. Newton, *Wasteland,* 56.

38. Newton, *Wasteland,* 67.

39. Newton, *Wasteland,* 146.

40. Newton, *Wasteland,* 55–56.

41. J. G. Ballard, *Cocaine Nights* (London: Flamingo, 1996), 180–181.

42. Chuck Palahniuk, *Fight Club* (New York: Henry Holt, 1999), 49.

43. Michel Houellebecq, *Whatever,* trans. Paul Hammond (London: Serpent's Tail, 1998), 30.

CHAPTER 3

The Crime System

Murder by Numbers

True crime is then a popular genre of our contemporary wound culture.[1] The style of violence it posits everywhere makes visible the media apriori. And the style of sociality it posits is, along these lines, commiseration: referred pain and referred belief.

That bond of togetherness—whether valued as the basis of an identity politics or devalued as a debased victim culture—is, however, difficult exactly to locate. The mass identifications, the specular transitivisms, that make up something like a social bond are at least as complex as the vicissitudes of identification at the level of the individual. These identificatory relays, however, tend to be simplified beyond recognition—and not least in accounts of the reality constructions of the mass media and in accounts of the effects of kinds of fictional violence on kinds of factual violence. On one level, there is nothing new about these concerns. From at least the seventeenth century on, narrative literature insistently reflects on the effects of literature just as novels insistently reappear in novels, cautioning about the effects of reading novels and about the risks to behavior as a consequence of print. The distinction between real and fictional reality is made from inside fiction, as the phrase "real life" itself comes from a novel (by the eighteenth-century novelist Richardson).[2]

Literature both effected this change and exposed it, as the mass media today endlessly reflect back on the truth or consequences of the mass media. These complications in the social reflex-ivity of intimate and social relationships have a long history. And these complications may appear then as a local case in the more general turn that has come to be called "reflexive modernity"—one version of what has also been called the "linguistic turn" or "cultural turn" in the understand-ing of what makes up society and the individuality of the individual.[3]

But what exactly does it mean when these complications become utterly explicit, and not least on the level of popular genres such as true crime? Reflecting on the reality of the mass media and its constructions, the systems theorist Niklas Luhmann concludes: "*How* is it possible to accept information about the world and about society as information about reality when one knows *how* it is constructed?"[4] Put simply: we may know that make believe makes belief, but can we then still believe it?[5]

These are large questions. The problem is that they have also come to look like empty ones. Consider, for example, this scene in the recent film *Murder by Numbers*. The police question a teenage murder suspect about the paper he's given in school, a paper about violence that might be described as "kind of Nietzschean." He is asked: "Do you believe it?" His response is simple enough: "It's a school paper, you have to write about something." It is not exactly the case that the student is merely disavowing belief in what he wrote, and hence making believe that he's innocent. In attesting that what he wrote was simply more or less what school papers are supposed to look like—in this case, some portentous pop-philosophi-cal clichés about killing and the will to power—he is attesting as well to the relays among clichés, canons of credibility, and modern violence. For, after all, "murder by numbers" refers not just to the number of victims that make a killer a serial killer and refers not just to how the "anonymiza-tion" of victims as numbers forms part of this modern style of violence. "Murder by numbers" is also something like "painting by numbers." It is an acting by rote and by code—albeit, of course, in the name of just the opposite, in the name of the freedom of art, and, here not least, of murder as one of those fine arts. It is, however, an acting by code precisely when that code has become utterly explicit.

The film *Murder by Numbers* loosely refers back to Hitchcock's *Rope*, which refers back to the Leopold and Loeb murder case, which in turn looked like a real case of Nietzsche-by-numbers. These ceaseless migrations across the fact/fiction divide trace the shape of belief in contemporary culture: the suspensions of belief and of disbelief, the conditions of plausibility and credibility, and the ways they are distributed socially, that true crime and false crime center on—and, in centering on them, as part of their "human interest" appeal, allow readers and viewers to try out for themselves.

Modern violence, along these lines, is reflexive violence. And one sign of this reflexivity is the reentry of observations and representations of violence into the interior of acts of violence; beliefs about crime and violence loop back on the kinds of violence and crime that then may take place just as beliefs about kinds of persons loop back on the kinds of things persons can do and be. To call this "social construction" is to enter the same sort of loop: it might go without saying that things that could only exist in the context of a society are social.[6] And this *strict socialization of the social,* it will emerge, is utterly crucial in understanding the utterly "system-like" character of modern crime and its popular representations.[7] The locked room of the classic detective story is nothing but a scale model of the closure of the social order, an order that makes itself from itself.

But this as yet tells us little more than that modern violence participates in the protocols of reflexive modernity, just like everything else that is modern about modernity—which means that the particular forms of that reflexivity, in the popular genres of wound culture such as true crime, remain to be set out. And the particular style of belief—or half-belief—that such unremittingly reflexive and transparent and yet effective forms put in places remains to be specified too.

It might be said that the high school killer in the film *Murder by Numbers* believes in what he wrote in the way that the contemporary gothic believes in its fear factor. If the model for the first is "Believe, kind of believe," the model for the second might be taken from the most popular contemporary survival of the gothic subgenre, the supernatural explained—that is, the animated pop-gothic Scooby-Doo, and its slogan, "Be afraid, be kind of afraid."

But what exactly do these half-beliefs and make-believe fears mean, then, in the making up of our contemporary pathological public sphere? We know that really believing one's beliefs disqualifies those beliefs. Really believing one's beliefs makes one a true believer. And the true believer, one who believes directly rather than obliquely, is at once stigmatized and pathologized *as* the true believer, the fanatic or fundamentalist. This is perhaps why the common way of ratifying shared belief is to share in the suspension of direct belief. Hence, an American typically affirms belief in something by saying what seems to be exactly the opposite: by saying "It's really unbelievable, isn't it?" The working model here might be the moment in *The Wizard of Oz* when the curtain is drawn back to expose the wizard and his mechanisms of illusion. His response of course is simply to say, "Pay no attention to the man behind the curtain!" This may be paradoxical. But the point not to be missed is that it works. The fiction seen through from both sides nonetheless survives this transparency and keeps going. One gets brains, courage, heart, and home anyway.

There is nothing uncanny in this referred or displaced belief. It indicates the social and hence mediated character of belief: one believes with and through the like-minded others with whom one shares this claim.[8] (Referred belief—a species of secondhand nonexperience—remains "uncanny" to the extent that it is reduced to a symptom of the contemporary incredulity with respect to the reality of the social bond or collective life.) Hence affirmations of referred belief are like talking about the weather. This is not, of course, a matter of conveying information or communicating something (say, "Look! It's raining!"). It is a matter of communicating communicativeness, of keeping ongoing the style of minimal sociality among strangers who may have in common only their commonness. In true crime and in its counterpart fictional genre, pulp fiction, there is a lot of weather and the weather is always bad. And since weather indexes what is left of nature—what is left to mark the limit or "outside" of the social order as an order and a system, making itself from itself—this heavy weather is also a way of marking the intramural and reflexive working of society-as-system (the emergence of, and sequestration of, "the social" as such).[9]

This may be enough to set out, in very preliminary ways, the styles of sociality and belief, and the relays between social and fictional forms, that true crime effects and exposes. These are the states of half-belief that Edgar Allan Poe, in his inaugural true crime fiction "The Mystery of

Marie Roget," calls "half-credences." Poe's tale has been described as "the first detective story in which an attempt was made to solve a real crime."[10] The fictional story can solve a real crime because, for Poe, crime operates according to a calculus of probabilities; crime, that is, works like a system. For Poe, among others, the death of God leaves us with mathematics and the death of Satan leaves us with forensics. Poe's version of forensic realism, his version of murder by numbers, will make it possible for us to take this account of true crime a step or two further. In the pages that follow I want first to look at the half-credences of Poe's tale: the social order it makes legible and credible and the style of sociality to which it acclimatizes a reading public. I want second to take up some of the larger implications, for historical work and literary work and for the relays between them, of the reflexive structure of publicness, belief, and crime that Poe's story begins to make visible. This will entail a look at the public codifications of intimacy, particularly in print and letters form, that run through both true crime and its counterpart genre, true romance. In subsequent parts, I consider how crime, true and false, has its place in what has come to be called the "risk society." It is, for the moment, something like the advent of those social conditions that concerns me here.[11]

Half-Credences; or, the Public Mind

"The Mystery of Marie Roget" is about the mysterious and brutal death, in New York in 1841, of a young woman, "The Beautiful Cigar Girl," named Mary Rogers. Poe's story consists largely of long passages taken almost verbatim from the daily press coverage of the case. But the story consists, more precisely, of a perverse transposition. In the forensic inquiry that for the most part makes up the story, Poe, point by point, transposes characters and events from the real New York—that is, the real New York of the penny papers—to a fictional Paris. In the "editorial" apparatus that runs the length of the story, he transposes them back. This is again a fiction seen through from both sides. But what exactly does this transparently fabricated illusion mean? And why does Poe think that this make-believe is a good way to go about solving a real crime?

About the death of Mary Rogers and its aftermath, the "popular excitement … which had so agitated the public mind," Poe writes: "I can call to mind no similar occurrence producing so general and so intense an effect" (Marie Roget, pp. 727–728, 726). This description of popular excitement could not be more exact. What makes it possible for this intensity to be *general* is the mass observation of violence via the print media. What makes it possible for this generality to be *intense* is the sensation of observing violence among an indeterminate number of other like-minded observers. That is, generality and intensity solicit, and feed on, each other. What becomes visible here, in the relays between violence and its mass observation, is then something like a new *intensity of reflexivity*.

Hence it is not merely then that "a new press, in the midst of finding a popular language to address its new and diverse audience, adopted a discourse of sensation that depended on images of death, of sexual violation, and the decomposition of the female form."[12] Nor is it merely a matter of the public exposure of private life or, beyond that, what Amy Gilman Srebnick, in her richly informed history of the death of Mary Rogers and its media, calls the "criminalization of private life."[13] It is possible here to speak of a media-dependent public sphere, if one understands this in terms of the collateral emergence of the public sphere (what Poe calls "the public mind") and mass print culture (the "public prints"). In systems-theoretical terms, we can describe this as the "double-contingency" of print and publicness. And this is what makes it possible for the mass spectacle of death to be both general and intense, anonymized and individualized, generic and singular, at once: both sensational *media* and a media *sensation*.

This is perhaps clearest in the popular way of understanding the mutual solicitation of print and publicness called *public opinion*. "In our country," William Gilmore Simms noted in 1856, "a great many crimes are committed to gratify public expectation … to satisfy the demands of public opinion, … [crimes] instigated by half-witted journalists, who first goad the offender to his crime, and, the next day, rate him soundly for his commission."[14] The sensational novelist George Lippard, writing in 1844, concisely instances what David Brion Davis has described as these intricate mechanisms of projected and vicarious aggression: the public mass spectacle of violence "aroused the public's taste for blood, increasing the incidence of violent crimes."[15] The self-observation of "public opinion" is thus a more effective—if necessarily more exposed—observation of the observation of others, via the mass media.[16] The press, along these lines, routinely takes up the "interest" in crime it instigates. "It is not to be wondered at," the New York *Transcript* reports in the matter of the sensational murder of Helen Jewett in 1836, "that such an excitement does exist as was manifested in every part of the city yesterday, in relation to this dreadful and almost unparalleled atrocity."[17] The press, it appears, never ceases not wondering about the nine days' wonders it wonders about. As Patricia Cline Cohen traces in detail, in her history of the murder of Helen Jewett (a case with many media parallels to that of Mary Rogers), the early 1830s New York press "pioneered the concept of a penny paper reporting on lively human interest stories"; in the Jewett case, as in the Rogers one, "the upstart penny press whipped up public interest, sustained a high level of enthusiasm over many months ... without the competition of the press, interest in the case would probably have sputtered in a short time."[18]

This means that the new market in "lively human interest stories"—centered on stories of sex, crime, and, above all, sex crime—indicates something more than the lurid self-promotion of the public prints. The press, it would seem, is in the business of generating interest in human interest. This is not difficult since an interest already exists to be drawn on, one that since the advent of the printing press has been of a general nature: namely, the interest in reading.[19] More exactly, the new penny press is in the business of generating "lively" (or lifelike) human interest as a particularized mass interest (general interest in this particular crime) and the popular interest as an excitedly reflexive formation of publicness (indissociable from mass mediation and crime both).

Poe's mystery story presents exactly these intricate mechanisms of popular opinion. But he represents them exactly in reverse. The shifting on its axis of popular opinion makes, for Poe and beyond, an understanding of the novelty of modern crime as involving something more than a critique of the media construction of reality and something more than an acknowledgment of a sort of generically "modernist" self-consciousness or self-problematization. It includes both of these things but is not reducible to either of them. It makes, in short, for the *understanding of crime as a social system* and for the understanding of the dependence of that system on the half-credences that make a public mind, or a social bond, possible.

Here, then, is the reverse-theory of popular opinion set out by Poe's detective Dupin:

> Now the popular opinion, under certain conditions, is not to be disregarded. When arising of itself—when manifesting itself in a strictly spontaneous manner—we should look upon it as analogous with that *intuition* which is the idiosyncrasy of the individual man of genius. In ninety-nine cases from the hundred I would abide by its decision. But it is important that we find no palpable traces of *suggestion.* The opinion must be rigorously *the public's own;* and the distinction is often exceedingly difficult to perceive and to maintain. In the present instance, it appears to me that this "public opinion," in respect to a *gang,* has been superinduced by the collateral event which is detailed in the third of my extracts. ("Marie Roget," p. 757)

This passage transparently inverts the belief conditions of the public and does so in at least three ways. For one thing, the entire investigation in "The Mystery of Marie Roget" proceeds by way of a reading of the public prints. But here "popular opinion," the public mind "of itself," is represented as "rigorously" immune to just those conditions, the technical and media conditions, on which it depends: the "superinduction" of public self-reflection. For another, the terms of "spontaneous" sociality—suggestion, influence, and intuition, for example—anticipate (as they resist) precisely the terms by which, by the end of the century, the mystery of group psychology and the social bond (the social substance, or what Tarde calls "the energy of social cohesion") will be understood: imitation, suggestion, hypnosis, energy, charisma, and so on. This (it will be seen in a moment) posits something like the counterfactual or *fictional* status of the social order. Hence, in Tarde's terms again, the impalpability and evanescence of the "social self"—its, as it were, phantom character—means that "the social, like the hypnotic state, is only a form of a dream."[20]

But here again, this dream state is, from the start of Poe's story, seen very differently. The point not to be missed here is that what makes for "spontaneous" sociality in Poe's account is not this dream state but instead state numbers—statistics. For if "in ninety-nine cases from the hundred" public opinion is rigorously the public's own, this is because events, or persons, or groups, understood *as* cases, are precisely calculable. Under modern social conditions, numbers—the law of large numbers and the calculus of probabilities—replace substance. Numbers, that is, make up those conditions.[21]

It is not hard to see that the calculus of probabilities informs Poe's story, not least in that "The Mystery of Marie Roget" begins and ends, it may be recalled, with a small lesson in that calculus. These are lessons about the inverse relation between popular opinion and mathematical truth. But, it may be recalled too, that the lessons are transparently false: popular fiction and mathematical fact in effect change places. It is necessary to look in some detail at what Poe's evocation of the conjectural sciences looks like here and what it can tell us about the logic of this true crime fiction.

Here is the example that Poe provides at the end of the story (holding "in view the very Calculus of Probabilities to which I have referred"):

> Nothing, for example, is more difficult than to convince the merely general reader that the fact of sixes having been thrown twice in succession by a player at dice, is sufficient cause for betting the largest odds that sixes will not be thrown in the third attempt. A suggestion to this effect is usually rejected by the intellect at once. It does not appear that the two throws which have been completed, and which lie now absolutely in the Past, can have influence upon the throw which exists only in the Future. The chance for throwing sixes seems to be precisely as it was at any ordinary time. ("Marie Roget," p. 773)

Exactly the opposite, of course, is the case. The "merely general reader" assumes precisely the "influence" of past on future tosses of the dice (a version of what is commonly known as "the gambler's fallacy"); in reality—that is, in mathematical reality—the odds of each toss remain exactly the same, regardless of the history of tosses. The reversal of positions means that the merely general reader believes in the strict individuality of each chance, whereas the truth is falsely asserted to lie with an "influence" on chances—a "vague" and "supernatural" influence that Poe opens his story by describing in terms of popular "half-credences" about coincidences. "There are few persons," Poe begins,

> even among the calmest thinkers, who have not occasionally been startled into a vague yet thrilling half-credence in the supernatural, by *coincidences* of so seemingly marvelous a character that, as *mere* coincidences, the intellect has been unable to receive them. Such sentiments—for the half-credences of which I speak have never the full force of *thought*—are seldom thoroughly stifled unless by reference to the doctrine of chance, or, as it is technically termed, the Calculus of Probabilities. ("Marie Roget," pp. 723–724)

And here Poe introduces the doctrine of chance, which will resolve into an intelligible system "the extraordinary details which I am now called upon to make public."[22]

Now there is little doubt that Poe knew he was shifting the places of the merely general reader and the "philosophical" one. There has then remained a good deal of doubt, however, as to what this transparent inversion of popular belief and the "purely mathematical" doctrine of chance means.[23] But it makes a good deal of sense if we consider the larger field of relations, social and fictional, in which the calculus of probability—and the conjectural sciences more generally—become visible, intelligible, and compelling.

The collateral development of the social sciences and the conjectural sciences could not be more evident: the central role, from the eighteenth century on, of statistics and probability, not merely in the management of social life but also in the conceptualization of "the social" as such. The "taming of chance," as Ian Hacking has traced in detail, "was intimately connected with larger questions about what a society is."[24] But what may be less evident is just how sociality refers back to the law of large numbers and how the half-credences that make up fiction refer back to both.

The intent here is not to take up, once again, the artificiality of the distinction between fiction and reality (an artificiality that becomes clear if we consider the difficulty of making and promoting it in the "factual fictions," the authentic true novels, of the seventeenth and earlier eighteenth centuries).[25] Nor is the intent to take up, once again, "the history of the modern fact," and its place, for example, in the perception of money and nations as self-regulating systems.[26] Nor is the intent even to take up, once again, links between fictional forms and the taming of chance and the accident. (As Poe puts it: "*Accident* is admitted as a portion of the substructure. We make chance a matter of absolute calculation" ["Marie Roget," p. 752]). In the most general terms, there is nothing new in the distinction between fiction and history, along these lines. Historical events, we know, are real but accidental; fictional events are unreal but essential. If this distinction seems a timeless one, it nevertheless takes on new forms of life—for example, in the question historical analysts keep asking as to whether history should take a "linguistic turn" or a "cultural turn." If the strict "socialization of society" that marks modernity involves precisely such a reflexive turn, then this question might more properly be framed as, Should historical studies take a historical turn?

These are questions about credibility, too (and the manner in which such difficulties are acknowledged in "interdisciplinary" work reminds us how acknowledging a difficulty may be one way of obviating dealing with it). Put simply, fiction (that is, factual fiction) and statistics emerge at roughly the same time, as two communicating versions of counterfactual reality. As Niklas Luhmann indicates, albeit without quite elaborating, in his *Art as a Social System:* "But what are we to make of the fact that the world is now divided into two kinds of reality—a world of singular events and a world of statistics (or of inductive references), a reality out there and a fictional reality?"[27] And, along the same lines, what is the "substructure" of popular or general belief that the division between these two realities, and their media, support? The intent here then is to trace the relays between numbers, society, and fiction—and not least between the "merely general" or mass reader and the general or mass belief in individuals and their singularity. These are the elementary particles that make up the crime system.

True Lies

It does not take much effort to see that the reflexive turn is central to the detective story and its reading protocols. Poe's detective Dupin, for example, observes obliquely, not directly (hence his ubiquitous "green shades"). That is, Poe's detective not exactly observes but observes observers observing. The story not merely consists for the most part of verbatim transcriptions from the newspapers; it consists largely of a rereading of the press and a rereading of its readings. Poe's detective, in this story, reads readers and reads what readers do not read. Among these readers is the criminal himself, who press-gangs the press into a tactical reworking of information about the case: "Here the [criminal's] well written and urgent communications to the journals are much in the way of corroboration" ("Marie Roget," p. 769). (And, as we will see in a moment, the ostensible scene of the crime is an artifact of the projected press coverage of the case as well.) What these communications corroborate is not simply Dupin's construction of the case, then, but its intensely reflexive turn. On this logic of observing and reading, as Poe's internal reader Dupin expresses it: "Queries, skillfully directed, will not fail to solicit, from some of these parties, information on this particular point (or upon others)—information which the parties themselves may not even be aware of possessing" ("Marie Roget," p. 770).

There is perhaps by now nothing extraordinary about this way of reading or detecting. No doubt the training manual for this sort of observation of observation is the novel itself. For one thing, the novel from the start describes behavior as a consequence of reading, which means that the plane of observation and the plane of action are in effect folded back onto each other.[28] For another, the two primary forms of the novel, the detective novel and the epistolary novel, taught one how to observe oneself and others as an observer, to read over the other's (and over one's own) shoulder. In short, this sort of reflexivity or "constructivism describes the observation of observation that concentrates on how the observed observer observes. This constructivist turn makes possible a qualitative change, a radical transformation, in the style of recursive observation, since by this means one can also observe what and how an observed observer is *un*able to observe."[29]

On this logic, the novel acclimatizes individuals (that is, readers) to the social demands of reflexivity. But the point not to be missed is that readers in the novel and readers of the novel understand this demand exactly in reverse: as the precipitation of a self-reflexivity and a self-consciousness—a training in individualization—that sets individuals directly at odds with social demands. Self-reflexivity is a warmer notion than reflexivity, and self-consciousness warmer still. The novel, as it were, psychologizes reflexivity (which has nothing to do with psychology or self-consciousness[30]), opening an endless dilemma. This dilemma, to the very extent that it can never be solved, can then take on the form, and support, of an endless problematization, which, in turn, can be taken to define what we mean by art.[31] Put simply, the society that makes itself from itself demands individuals who make themselves from themselves, which means that the social imperative of self-making is experienced exactly in reverse: as an unremitting war between two large abstractions, "self" and "society."[32]

Here one can begin to locate what the condition of the "merely general reader" who holds out for individuality looks like. And one can begin to locate the significance of sensational stories of sex and crime, and the sex crime, in scripting that individuality. Poe's detective story, among others, is premised on the anonymization of strangers in modern urban conditions ("numerous individuals" among "the entire population of Paris itself" ["Marie Roget," p. 750]). It is premised on the forensic case-likeness of this *ordinary, although atrocious instance of crime"* (on "the great frequency, in large cities of such atrocities as the one described" and on what he insistently calls "the human body in general" ["Marie Roget," pp. 736, 727, 741]). On this view, the "popular mind" and "public emotion" seem to require, as a sort of antidote, abnormality or pathology: "prominences above the plane of the ordinary" ("Marie Roget," p. 736). If, as Poe concisely puts it, "nothing is more vague than impressions of individual identity," pathology thus seems to provide the conditions for individualization ("Marie Roget," p. 748).

But this is a bit misleading. There is something more at stake here than an individualizing deviance or criminality—and not least if deviance and crime themselves are admitted as "a portion of the substructure" and made "a matter of absolute calculation." "The cardinal concept of psychology of the Enlightenment had been," Ian Hacking observes, "simply human nature. By the end of the nineteenth century, it was being replaced by something different: normal people."[33] But the problem is that people like you and me are just like you and me. And this paradox (the yielding of identity to identification) erupts in violence, what I have described as the *violence–normality complex.*[34]

The extremes of personalization and anonymization communicate directly with each other. Hence "the temptation to narcissism is all the more seductive here in that it seems to express the common law: do as others do to be yourself."[35] Each man imitates the each for each of the other. These paradoxes operate throughout earlier American homicide fiction. If, for example, "the bonds of sympathetic identification" secure social law, the imperative of individualization means that one must make oneself "a law unto himself." And if the socialization of society means that the criminal is nothing but a reflex of his context ("circumstances make guilt"), this means in turn that compulsion and motiveless violence are paradoxically turned round into evidence of a radical freedom: the passivity of passion experienced as action at the extreme, and as a violent denial of self-limits. Motiveless crime—which should signal the subject no longer answerable as a subject—thus becomes just the opposite: the last reserve of the subject without a cause, that is, the subject as such.[36]

And there is a direct communication too between the logic of the victim and a radical egoism. If the subject, as in contemporary victim culture, grounds his speech on his status as a victim of circumstances beyond his control, this traumatized subject is also the subject as a law unto himself: the victim subject is also the extreme narcissist. For the notion of the subject as an irresponsible victim involves "the extreme Narcissistic perspective from which every encounter with the Other appears as a potential threat to the subject's precarious imaginary balance." In this way, "the self-centered assertion of the psychological subject paradoxically overlaps with the perception of oneself as a victim of circumstances."[37]

These tensions and paradoxes are, of course, the terrain of fiction itself, which, in the most general terms, tells about types or cases learning to think of themselves as individuals—learning to observe others and themselves and to make themselves—while it invites readers to do the same. Sex and crime are the preferred topics for playing out these tensions, and not merely then because these deviations above, or below, the ordinary have a lurid attraction. Beyond that, these topics make it possible to map in high relief these processes of individualization (latent and suppressed motives, decisions and indecisions, the life histories they make up, the *Bildung* thing generally, and so forth). If murder is where bodies and histories cross, the sex crime is where the extremes of individualization and socialization meet and fuse. True crime, the life histories of infamous men, melodramatizes these topics and tensions. The ordinary and merely general reader can thus entertain processes of individualization, while he reflects on the distinctions, and links, between normality and deviancy, which reflection is, in turn, a critical part of those processes.

These ties between the novel and itineraries of individualization are perhaps familiar enough. They are some of the ways true crime acclimatizes readers to, and interests them in, the social demands of reflexivity. One learns about individuality and intimacy in books (while also learning there that they are not the sort of thing one can learn in books). This is part of that strange mixture of awareness and credulity called "the willing suspension of disbelief." Again, one not merely knows but knows that one knows, and it works anyway. This "anyway" (or, now, "Whatever!") is more named than explained by generalizing notions of, say, "disavowal." Knowingness is, after all, both the condition and the effect of these reflexive protocols: these half-beliefs or half-credences.

Referred belief is thus a version of putting oneself in the place of the other. Putting oneself in the place of the other (sympathetic identification) becomes necessary when the other's place becomes in effect a replaceable part—a placeholder for any number of others. That is, that place no longer depends on the model of face-to-face interaction and its codes but is opened to an indeterminate number of semistrangers, those who are near but also far. (To the extent that empathy or sympathetic identification is observed, for example, in novels, the ultimate criterion becomes, Does the observing succeed in seducing someone to observe?[38]) As economic thought becomes a conjectural science of possible anticipations and combinations, and as communication in print culture becomes the structural condition of anonymized and probable readers, structure and system (the invisible hand, the calculus of probabilities, the merely general reader) replace interaction.[39]

It is not surprising, then, that putting oneself in the other's place is, from Poe on, the formal principle of detection in crime writing. As Poe expresses it in "The Murders in the Rue Morgue": "Deprived of ordinary resources, the analyst throws himself into the spirit of his opponent, identifies himself therewith."[40] (This, it may be noted, remains the method of the contemporary superdetectives called "profilers"—who, like Poe, combine statistical pictures of the criminal with a gothicized identification.) Nor should it be surprising by now that the problem of belief is not merely italicized by its repetition in Poe's "The Mystery of Marie Roget" but that believing and disbelieving, half-credences, are analyzed precisely as the problem of the other's belief and of making others believe.

Here then is Dupin's analysis of referred belief, by way of a reading of the situation of an initial suspect-witness in the Roget case, M. Beauvais:

> "He persists," says the paper, "in asserting the corpse to be that of Marie, but cannot give a circumstance … to make others believe." Now, without readverting to the fact that stronger evidence "to make others believe," could *never* have been adduced, it may be remarked that a man may very well be understood to believe, in a case of this kind, without the ability to advance a single reason for the belief of a second party. Nothing is more vague than impressions of individual identity. Each man recognizes his neighbor, yet there are few instances in which any one is prepared to *give a reason* for his recognition. The editor of L'Etoile had no right to be offended at M. Beauvais' unreasoning belief. ("Marie Roget," p. 748)

Poe first quotes from the newspapers—"to make others believe"—and then quotes his quotation. This registers in miniature what is at issue in the sociality of referred belief. For one thing, quotation (as we have seen) is the most economical way of making someone believe: one is invited, or coerced, into believing because one hears, or reads, that someone else somewhere else believes it.[41] In this way, that belief is always "the belief of a second party." For another, if nothing is vaguer than impressions of individual identity, this is because one believes, and thus recognizes, one's neighbor as oneself. The semistrangers in the great metropolis called "neighbors"—any number of whom may read the same papers and any number of whom (like contemporary viewers of CNN) may then regard themselves as being "the first to know"—share in the unreasoning beliefs that indicate the common place that they share in common.

There is one final turn here in the matter of making others believe, in that making others believe is nothing but what making up fictions does. "Let us pursue our fancies. ... We may imagine her thinking thus" ("Marie Roget," pp. 771, 756). Forensics in Poe's true crime fiction necessarily gives way to fancies, imaginings, and conjectures. The detective not merely conjectures what must have taken place but conjectures what the victim and suspects must have conjectured. "A dozen times he hears or fancies the steps of an observer. ... She must have thought of these things, I say. She must have foreseen the ... suspicion of all" ("Marie Roget," pp. 764, 756). Beyond that, the detective makes up small counterfactual scenes—little fictions—that must have taken place. Hence, Marie is imagined thinking thus: "I am to meet a certain person for the purpose of elopement. ... It is necessary that there be no chance of interruption. ... I will give it to be understood that I shall visit and spend the day with my aunt. ... If I bid St. Eustache call for me at dark ... if I wholly neglect to bid him call ... if it were my design to return at all ... he will be *sure* to ascertain that I have played him false" ("Marie Roget," p. 756) and so on. Inset within (that is, *quoted* within) the forensic analyses of "The Mystery of Marie Roget," these small scenes are little counterfactual fictions—true lies. Public facts precipitate fictions that test out, in turn, how the true crime system works.

These scenes are, more exactly, conjectural reenactments. Such reenactments are, of course, one of the staples of true crime, from Poe to *America's Most Wanted*. But the point is that these scenes are not merely a way of dramatizing the evidence. Reenactment is a necessary component in the recursive and reflexive structure of modern crime (as is its counterpart notion—the popular, and dubious, presumption of "the return to the scene of the crime"). The real point is that Poe's observer does not simply conjecture what the victim or suspect might have thought or done. These individuals are imagined as performing exactly the same operation: calculating, hypothesizing, ascertaining, making things up, and anticipating their effects. Interior states are thus seen precisely as scenes of conjecture, observing observing, and making believe. Interior states look like conjectural thinking, which looks like fiction. For this reason, it makes no sense to speak of the "influence" of the calculus of probabilities on fiction. It makes no sense to do so because these two counterfactual ways of believing are, if not two ways of saying the same thing, mutually contingent, referring back to each at every point.[42]

True Romance

If interior states look like fiction, this reflects what has been described as the social reflexivity of intimacy. The complication of course is that intimacy is required to be neither social nor reflexive: it is required to be natural. For if we know that we love and suffer according to social or cultural scripts, we know too that love and pain are taken to mark the limit point of the social and cultural. (Hence, the popular appeal of the trauma thing and the Lacanian Real—the point at which the social-symbolic order is seen to break down: one can, in this way, be theoretical and touch "the real" too.) One must know how to make love and know not least that love is not something that can be made. For this reason, the question "Who wrote the book of love?" cannot merely remain a rhetorical one but continue to work as a love song, much as mass-produced greeting cards can copy phrases and compliments without being simply taken as fabricated or tactless.[43]

These obvious dilemmas as to the genuineness of feelings are of course the dilemmas of love stories, which cannot cease exposing the genuineness or naturalness they sponsor. This is perhaps clearest in contemporary books of love such as Masters and Johnson's *Human Sexual Inadequacy*, which treats, among other things, the "spectator role" that enters into "fears of performance": "Whereas the whole therapy continually creates a consciousness of performance or inadequate performance (or at least can hardly avoid doing so), the resulting observation of oneself and others is seen as a weighty barrier to performance."[44] Like romantic irony or the well-rehearsed problem of the confessional or the genre-fictions of love and courtship, stimulation and precaution, or simulation, are coupled together at every point. One might, of course, move from performance anxiety to something like an endorsement of performativity, as a way of moving beyond this dilemma. But it is not exactly clear that there is much of an advantage in trading in performance anxiety for performativity anxiety—trading in the fear that one is not performing well enough for the fear that one is not being performative (or deconstructive) enough.

Nor is there, I think, much of an advantage in the reverse strategy: the historian's move to obviate the cultural or linguistic turn, to move "beyond the cultural turn." This is by and large represented as a matter of incorporating "theoretical" challenges that "cannot be easily dismissed" and then (registering that) moving "beyond" them.[45] As the editors of the recent collection *Beyond the Cultural Turn* put it: "Although the authors in this collection have all been profoundly influenced by the cultural turn, they have refused to accept the obliteration of the social that is implied by the most radical forms of culturalism or poststructuralism."[46] The gesture here, toward but against theory, is by now a familiar one. But—even accepting the specter of such a radicalism (the twin specters of solipsism and relativism)—what exactly does the obliteration of the social mean here?

One author in the collection "reminds us," we are told, that "We must never forget to watch ourselves knowing the otherness of the past, but this is not the same as merely watching ourselves."[47] The problem is that the notion of "merely watching ourselves" makes no sense. If one acknowledges that identity is modeled on identification, self-reference on heteroreference—that is, if one watches and believes with and through others—then the danger is not that we would be only watching ourselves. The real danger—one *parried* by the specter of solipsism—is that watching ourselves in no way gets us "beyond" the paradoxes of observing and observing observing I have been indicating here. The real danger, that is, is not "mere" solipsism but its implausibility, which is to say, the *social* character of belief. The paradoxes of watching and observing do not obliterate the social: they are bound up through and through with the reflexive intensities of modern sociality (the socialization of society). It is, in these terms, the move "beyond" this paradoxicality (or, conversely, its fetishization) that, in effect, obliterates the specific character of the social in the name of attending to it.[48]

The cultural turn, in Poe's story, could not be more exact. Briefly, the "crime" in the case of Mary Rogers/Marie Roget turns out to be, not murder, but "An accident at Madame Deluc's" ("Marie Roget," p. 763), that is, a botched abortion that leads to the young woman's death. The accident is covered over by staging a simulated scene of the crime. That scene is outside the precincts of the city, but in a suburban setting that is less a place for "lovers of nature" than the already "polluted" scene of weekend wilding, a sort of nature theme park of "a counterfeit hilarity" (p. 760). The nature of the scene and the counterfeit and "highly artificial" arrangements of the evidence are represented in these terms:

> Within its naturally walled enclosure were three extraordinary stones, *forming a seat with a back and a footstool* … [in] this thicket, so full of natural art … a day never passed over the heads of these boys without finding at least one of them ensconced in the umbrageous hall, and enthroned upon its natural throne. … Here is just such an arrangement as would *naturally* be made by a not-over-acute person wishing to dispose the articles *naturally*. But it is by no means a *really* natural arrangement. ("Marie Roget," pp. 761–762)

This kind of crime and this kind of crime scene are bound up through and through with the reflexive intensities of the crime system. Abortion here represents something like the end, or death, of nature—ex-nature. The extraordinary "natural art" of this artificial crime scene represents its socialization. And the socialization of nature signals precisely the sequestration of social and intimate relations, which, we have seen, is the scene and condition of true crime.

But if interior states in true crime look like fiction, it is possible to specify further what exactly this means and to take up some of its larger implications. Consider, for example, an instance of contemporary academic true crime, Patricia Cline Cohen's recent account of a case that has (as I have indicated) strong resemblances to the case of Mary Rogers and its media sensationalism: the murder of Helen Jewett, the prostitute victim of an axe-murder in New York in 1836. The study begins with this sentence: "April 9 of 1836 was an unseasonably cold Saturday night in New York City, coming at the end of the coldest and longest winter of the early nineteenth century."[49] Academic true crime reads like bad fiction too. The weather report (again, the residue of nature) thus necessarily gives way at once to a strictly social-historical account of the murder: the report is followed by a two-page reproduction of a detailed street map of early nineteenth-century lower Manhattan. Cohen's intent is to "thickly" situate the case, such that it provides an index of social and cultural conditions of period and place. Hence, for the historian Cohen too, nothing is vaguer than impressions of individual identity: for example, the main suspect in the unsolved case, Robinson, "Seemed indistinguishable from thousands of other similarly situated young clerks" (*Helen Jewett*, p. 22). Their typical situation, along with that of prostitutes, brothel keepers, newsmen, among other social types, is set out in forensic detail. One situates the murder in the supersaturated social context of early New York such that the event becomes a transparency that, in circular fashion, discloses that context: sex and culture in nineteenth-century New York. Distinction yields to situation. And since the murder was and remains unsolved, there is no end, in this version of archive fever, to evidentiary contextualization. Or, as Freud noted somewhere, in a somewhat different context, "Now we know everything—except why the murder was committed."

The notion of situating the subject is of course by now something of a commonplace. But so too is the dubious topography of situating. This amounts to the internally conflicted notion that, in order to make sense of persons or events, it is necessary to "situate them historically," but that situating persons or events in effect evacuates them, such that they become nothing more than an effect or reflex of that situation. Put somewhat differently, true crime sets out the general social conditions of the crime, which the crime is then taken to illustrate. Persons and acts illustrate the conditions that make up the persons who act that way. (If the subject is social "all the way down"—if a person is something that can be made—then she is simply the subjective synonym of her objective construction—an individualized correlate of the world.)

It is surprising that one can continue to be surprised by this (or continue to offer it as a "discovery"). But the capacity to be surprised by it (to be surprised to find that one is digging up what one has just buried) may indicate the half-credences (the reflexive imperative) in play here as well. This is something like another game about interiority: the very young child who plays hide-and-seek by saying, "I'm going to hide here, now you try to find me." One might shorten this round trip. But that would eliminate the necessary detours in the direction of the *individualization* of those conditions and players, which is part of the interest of true crime and its fictional counterparts. These personalizations allow for points of identification and—in filling in life histories and motivational positions—script programs for individualization, general and prescriptive as they are.

"The murder," Cohen observes,

> provided an opportunity to talk and write about power relations between men and women. The subject was sex, an intimate topic normally beyond the frontiers of polite and public discussion. Under the guise of "news," literary and artistic depictions of the corpse itself—beautiful, naked, dead—presented material for erotic contemplation. (*Helen Jewett*, p. 21)

The point about this is not that Cohen's own account inevitably rehearses that same "opportunity," moral and feral at once, for talking or writing about sex, power, and intimacy in public. This reflexiveness (observing observers observe, public privacy, stranger-intimacy, and so on) should by now be self-evident. The recursive forms of modern intimacy are visible not merely in that, it is reported at the time, "the brothel teemed with spectators" (*Helen Jewett*, p. 14) and not merely in that this spectatorship, now in turn, becomes the material for further spectation and "contemplation." Helen Jewett is represented as representative and as a version of the "self-made woman." The presumption of social construction (the notion that persons are things that can be made, from the outside in) is coupled with the presumption of self-construction (self-making, from the inside out). This paradoxical coupling is both subject and effect of those training manuals in self-realization and the protocols of interiority and intimacy that include popular romantic literature and letters. And self-making, in the Jewett case, among others, is literally a matter of reading and writing: that is, a self-making, via absorption in this kind of popular writing. It is a matter of what Cohen calls epistolary enticement and what might be described as the postal unconscious.

Helen Jewett, the contemporary press reiterated, "passed for quite a literary character": "Jewett's character became a work of cheap romantic fiction ... she truly passed over the line into fiction," becoming one of an indefinite number of "true life seduction stories" (*Helen Jewett*, pp. 30, 357). The details are familiar enough. Jewett, we are told, worked to "fashion herself as a literary romantic" (p. 124) and this self-fashioning involved not merely the writing of romantic letters to her clients but the semipublic circulation of her private letters among her clients—letters that later, after the murder, found their way into the public prints (along with iconic engravings of Jewett on the public streets, sealed letter in hand). These private letters were from the start generic and public: "Mr. G. might well have thought that Helen Jewett copied her letter from some writing manual or school text of the day" (p. 124). School text or school paper: true romance looks like love by numbers, and stranger-intimacy is the condition of love by numbers and murder by numbers both.

There is more, along these lines. *La femme-copie*, Jewett drew one of her aliases from a popular Scottish (that is, "Scottish") romance and her bookshelves were lined with this sort of writing. The local press she read endlessly reflected on the effects of reading: self-reflective articles on the influence of novels and romances with titles like "The Influence of Novels and Romances on the Morals" (cited in *Helen Jewett*, p. 173). And novelizations of the Jewett case focused on her own reading habits and its effects (p. 179).

"Robinson's action in murdering Jewett," we are told, "remained incomprehensible" (*Helen Jewett*, p. 359). But "incomprehensible " means that its meaning is bound up through and through with general interpretive, even literary, activity—with literature and literature's media monopoly on love and intimacy. That is, "it lies buried and implicit in their extraordinary correspondence and in the other interviews and letters Robinson left to the world after his trial" (p. 359). His modus operandi, one speculates, may have come from a recently theatricalized novel about the murder of a young woman and the murderer's acquittal: "He—and the whole theatergoing town—had seen the play *Norman Leslie* at the Bowery in the winter of 1836; Jewett had recently read the book" (p. 360). And so on.

In short, "reading was all around young [Helen Jewett]. ... all around her" (*Helen Jewett*, pp. 177, 180). No doubt the case fits well into the context of the so-called reading revolution, from the 1820s on. By the early nineteenth century, we know, reading had become what the poet Lydia Huntley Sigourney called a "necessity of existence"[50] and what the novelist Catherine Maria Sedgwick called "the new 'reading world.'"[51] And the point not to be missed is that a reading world is a self-observing world.

But a series of very basic questions emerges at this point. For if reading is all around Jewett, if reading makes up her "context," what sort of context, after all, is *reading*? And what does it mean when the return to the scene of reading—by now, familiar enough—is also the return to the scene of the crime?

We have been tracing the style of sociality proper to a reading world— a world of merely general readers, interested in reading about individual readers like themselves. One rediscovers here the necessarily reflexive condition of reading and publicness alternatively described as the reading public and the public prints. And we have been tracing the pathologization of public space in a wound culture. This is a world in which, as we have seen, public space and the scene of the crime appear as two ways of saying the same thing. This is a world, that is, in which openness to another (intimacy) and openness to others (sociality) are experienced in terms of woundedness. This is the double logic of the pathological public sphere. The torn and open body, the torn and exposed psyche, becomes the measure of publicness (it will be recalled that *Öffentlichkeit*, Habermas's term for the public sphere, means openness). And, collaterally, publicness itself is criminalized or pathologized.

This should by now be clear enough, but its implications are perhaps less evident. I have elsewhere traced in some detail these loopings of publicness and woundedness, intimacy and violation.[52] These relations are nowhere clearer than in the matter of technology and, not least, media technologies. The fear of technological determinism is often a stand-in for a fear of mediation, and the fear of mediation is often a stand-in for a fear of relation, social and intimate. For this reason, the mass-media spectacle and violence, or violation, tend to indicate each other at every point—and this is the case regardless of the "content" of the spectacle. To the extent that the experience of mass mediation, at the level of the subject, becomes an experience of uncontrollable and thus insupportable openness, openness and intimacy are experienced as woundedness. Hence our everyday intimacies with technology, and not least media technologies, tend to be represented in reverse: as an unremitting hostility between "real" intimacy and technology. This is true both of true romance and true crime: the popular literature and spectacle of open and broken hearts and the popular literature and spectacle of torn and opened bodies.[53]

True romance, like true crime, at once assumes and exposes an unremitting literacy in affairs of the heart. The new reflexivities of a reading public, for example, hold steadily visible the strange materialities of writing and letters, whether scarlet letters or stolen ones.[54] They make visible, beyond that, the public media of love and intimacy and their protocols. Put simply, the link between literature and letters could not be more evident: the novel originates as private letters made public or, more exactly, as love letters designed or designated for interception. It is not merely that intimate secrets went to print (which is to say that intimacy and secrecy—and this is their open secret—circulated from the start *as* public discourse). Nor is it merely that, as I have noted, the two basic forms of narrative fiction—the detective story and the epistolary novel—both depend on the post: delivered, deferred, and (of course) purloined.[55]

Briefly, once it becomes possible to write on sheets of paper that can be folded back on themselves (rather than, say, rolled into a scroll), once it becomes possible for the handwritten and folded sheet of paper to be inserted in an envelope, sealed, and posted on schedule, the technical conditions of interiority and privacy are in place. That is, interiority and privacy are in place. At this point, it becomes possible for the writing of letters to get in the way of letters, for the technical conditions of intimacy to get in the way of intimacy. Love letters are, we know, largely self-references to the occasion, and scene, and genre of their writing and sending. Love can scarcely dispense with the rules and protocols of its communication, as private letters cannot cease referring to (literary) letters and as privacy cannot cease referring to its interception. Private life, and real life, are lived reflexively, bound not least to the emotions and observations preformed or prescribed in literature, and bound not least to the fiction, seen through from both sides, that we never cease not knowing that.

Notes

1. On the formation of a "wound culture" and pathological public sphere, see my *Serial Killers: Death and Life in America's Wound Culture* (New York: Routledge, 1998).
2. See Niklas Luhmann, *Love as Passion: The Codification of Intimacy*, trans. Jeremy Gaines and Doris L. Jones (Stanford, CA: Stanford University Press, 1988), 74.
3. On "reflexive modernity," see, for example, Niklas Luhmann, *Observations on Modernity*, trans. William Whobrey (Stanford, CA: Stanford University Press, 1998); Anthony Giddens, *The Consequences of Modernity* (Cambridge: Polity Press / Blackwell, 1990); Ulrich Beck, *The Risk Society: Towards a New Modernity*, trans. Mark Ritter (London: Sage, 1992).
4. See Niklas Luhmann, *The Reality of the Mass Media*, trans. Kathleen Cross (Stanford, CA: Stanford University Press, 2000), 74.
5. In the pages that follow it will become clear that I am here in part testing out what recent "systems theory," and in particular the work of its main theorist Niklas Luhmann, can tell us about true crime and its protocols. It will become clear too why the question as to whether systems theory provides a good account of the social conditions I will be examining—the conditions of "reflexive modernity"—or just a good symptom of them must remain unsettled.
6. On the "looping effects of human kinds," see Ian Hacking, *The Social Construction of What?* (Cambridge, MA: Harvard University Press, 2000). Limiting such looping effects, or recursivity, to "human kinds" in effect limits this account of social construction to psychic systems—to the order of the subject. This not merely obviates recognition of the social-systemic character of self-reflexivity (which has nothing to do with "the self"). It hesitates, in the name of the social construction of reality, as to the reality of social construction. Along these lines, social constructionism continues the "self

and society" paradox it means to resolve. Not surprisingly then, Hacking's testing out of social construction tends toward cases of psychic pathology (see, e.g., *Mad Travelers: Reflections on the Reality of Transient Mental Illnesses* [Charlottesville: University Press of Virginia, 1998]). Not surprisingly too, trauma theory today has become the preferred way of "toggling" between psychic and social orders, even as the connection between them is black-boxed. (On the trauma apriori in contemporary culture, see my "Berlin 2000: 'The Image of an Empty Place,'" in *After-Images of the City,* ed. Joan Ramon Resina and Dieter Ingenschay [Ithaca, NY: Cornell University Press, 2003], 61–74, a version of which appears in chapter 6, below.) I will return to this pathologization, and criminalization, of reflexivity in the pages that follow.

7. On "the socialization of society," see Henri Lefebvre, *Introduction to Modernity*, trans. John Moore (1962; London: Verso, 1995), 190; see also Claude Lefort, *Political Forms of Modern Society: Bureaucracy, Democracy, Totalitarianism,* ed. John B. Thompson (Cambridge, MA: MIT Press, 1986); *Democracy and Political Theory,* trans. David Macey (Minneapolis: University of Minnesota Press, 1988); and Giddens, *The Consequences of Modernity.*

8. Slavoj Žižek's work orbits the "uncanniness" of shared belief: see, for example, *The Plague of Fantasies* (New York: Verso, 1997): "In an uncanny way, belief always seems to function in the guise of 'belief at a distance'" (p. 108); see also Slavoj Žižek, *On Belief* (New York: Routledge, 2001), 109–110. But references to the uncanny function less as an explanation than as a placeholder for one, in effect "gothicizing" the social character of belief and registering the sociality of belief as a traumatic public "penetration" into the most intimate private sphere, a "plague" of fantasies. It registers the contemporary understanding of publicness as uncanny. Or, in Richard Sennett's terms, "Intimacy is an attempt to solve the public problem by denying that the public exists." Richard Sennett, *The Fall of Public Man* (1976; New York: Norton, 1992), 27.

9. On the "sequestration" of the social, see Anthony Giddens, *Modernity and Self-Identity* (Stanford, CA: Stanford University Press, 1991), 144–180.

10. Edgar Allan Poe, "The Mystery of Marie Roget," in *Tales and Sketches,* vol. 2, *1843–1848,* ed. Thomas Ollive Mabbott (Urbana: University of Illinois Press, 2000), 715. Subsequent references in text, abbreviated "Marie Roget."

11. It is less a matter here of "periodizing" reflexive modernity—periodization is, after all, a protocol of modernity—than in tracing the *contexts of intensification* in which true crime forms a part, and the specific conditions—here

centrally the *recursivity* of social and self-observation effected and exposed by an emergent mass media—that realize such intensification.

12. Amy Gilman Srebnick, *The Mysterious Death of Mary Rogers: Sex and Culture in Nineteenth-Century New York* (New York: Oxford University Press, 1995), 63. See also Patricia Cline Cohen, *The Murder of Helen Jewett: The Life and Death of a Prostitute in Nineteenth-Century New York* (New York: Knopf, 1998), subsequently referred to in the text as *Helen Jewett*; and Karen Halttunen, *Murder Most Foul: The Killer and the American Gothic Imagination* (Cambridge, MA: Harvard University Press, 1998).

13. Srebnick, *Mysterious Death of Mary Rogers,* 87.

14. William Gilmore Simms, *Beauchampe; or, The Kentucky Tragedy* (1842; New York: J. W. Lovell, 1856), 337–338; discussed in David Brion Davis, *Homicide in American Fiction: 1798–1860* (Ithaca, NY: Cornell University Press, 1957), 277.

15. George Lippard, *The Quaker City; or, The Monks of Monk Hall* (Philadelphia, 1845), 452

16. See Niklas Luhmann, *Theories of Distinction: Redescribing the Descriptions of Modernity,* ed. William Rasch (Stanford, CA: Stanford University Press 2002), 173–174; and Pierre Bourdieu, "Opinion Polls: A 'Science' without a Scientist," in *In Other Words: Essays toward Reflexive Sociology,* trans. Matthew Adamson (Stanford, CA: Stanford University Press, 1990), 168–174.

17. Transcript (April 12, 1836), cited in Cohen, *Murder of Helen Jewett,* 22.

18. Cohen, *Murder of Helen Jewett,* 13.

19. Luhmann, *Love as Passion,* 44.

20. Gabriel Tarde, *The Laws of Imitation*, trans. E. C. Parsons (1890; New York, 1903), 76–77. See also Tarde, "Belief and Desire," in *On Communication and Social Influence: Selected Papers of Gabriel Tarde,* ed. Terry N. Clark (Chicago: University of Chicago Press, 1969): "belief, no more than desire, is neither logically nor psychologically subsequent to sensation … far from arising out of an aggregate of sensations, belief is indispensable both to their formation and their arrangement" (pp. 197–198). Hence, for Tarde, it is not merely that mass media and the technical instruments of mass communication are central to social formation. Social life has its basis in the communicative relays of imitated or referred belief: that is to say, "the primacy of the means of communication over all the instruments of social life." See Serge Moscovici, *The Age of the Crowd: A Historical Treatise on Mass Psychology,* trans. J. C. Whitehouse (Cambridge: Cambridge University Press, 1985), 158; and Jonathan Crary, *Suspensions of Perception: Attention, Spectacle, and Modern Culture* (Cambridge, MA: MIT Press, 1999), 241–245.

21. On social numbers, see Lefort, *Democracy and Political Theory,* 18–19; on statistics and the individuality of the individual, see my "Statistical Persons," in *Bodies and Machines* (New York: Routledge, 1992); on numbers, privatization, and crime, Joan Copjec, "The Phenomenal Nonphenomenal: Private Space in *Film Noir,*" in *Shades of Noir,* ed. Joan Copjec (New York: Verso, 1993), 167–197.

22. "Make public," it should be clear by now, in both senses. Consider here a contemporary commentary on Poe's story "The Gold Bug": "The intent of the author was evidently to write a popular tale: money, and the finding of money, being chosen as the most popular thesis. In this he endeavored to carry out his idea of the perfection of the plot, which he defines as—that, in which nothing can be disarranged, or from which nothing can be removed, without ruin to the mass—as that, in which we are never able to determine whether any point depends upon or sustains any one other. ... The bug, which gives title to the story, is used only in the way of mystification, having throughout a seeming and no real connection with the subject. Its purpose is to seduce the reader into the idea of supernatural machinery and keeping him so mystified until the last moment" (Thomas Dunn [1845], quoted in Poe, *Tales and Sketches,* 799). The popular circulation of fiction, money, and readers thus indicate each other at every point, such that it becomes impossible, in the reciprocal and seductive process of circulation, to determine what determines what: in short, the "thesis" is the popular, and semiocculted, "machinery" of popularity—the popularity of popularity.

23. On mathematics in "The Mystery of Marie Roget," see John T. Irwin, *The Mystery to a Solution: Poe, Borges, and the Analytic Detective Story* (Baltimore: Johns Hopkins University Press, 1994), 321–330.

24. Ian Hacking, *The Taming of Chance* (Cambridge: Cambridge University Press, 1990), 7.

25. Cf. Niklas Luhmann, *Art as a Social System,* trans. Eva Knodt (Stanford, CA: Stanford University Press, 2000), 282, 313; and Niklas Luhmann, *Social Systems,* trans. John Bednarz Jr. with Dirk Baecker (Stanford, CA: Stanford University Press, 1995), 569–570.

26. Cf. Mary Poovey, *A History of the Modern Fact: Problems of Knowledge in the Sciences of Wealth and Society* (Chicago: University of Chicago Press, 1998).

27. Luhmann, *Art as a Social System,* 175; see also Luhmann, *Observations on Modernity:* "Modernity has invented probability calculations just in time to maintain a fictionally created, dual reality" (p. 70).

28. See Jonathan Ellmer, "Blinded Me with Science: Motifs of Observation and Temporality in Lacan and Luhmann," in *Observing Complexity: Systems Theory and Postmodernity,* ed. William Rasch and Cary Wolfe (Minneapolis: University of Minnesota Press, 2000), 215–246.

29. Luhmann, *Art as a Social System,* 265; see also Luhmann, *Observations on Modernity,* 19.

30. A thermostat, for example, is self-reflexive too: it is impossible to say whether the thermostat regulates the temperature of the room or the temperature of the room regulates the thermostat—but the thermostat does not stay up all night worrying about it.

31. See, for example, Luhmann, *Love as Passion,* 163.

32. For a more detailed account of this double imperative of social construction and self construction, and the manner in which it lends itself to spectacular public violence, see my *Serial Killers,* 105–124.

33. Hacking, *The Taming of Chance,* 1.

34. See my "The Conventions of True Crime: Technologies of Belief, Commiseration, Publicness," in *Nation as Narration: Media and Modernity* (Moscow, 2002), 148–161.

35. Marc Augé, *Non-Places: Introduction to an Anthropology of Supermodernity,* trans. John Howe (London: Verso, 1995), 106.

36. I am in part "sampling" the accounts of crime attribution set out in David Brion Davis, *Homicide in American Fiction, 1798–1860,* 257, 48, 75–76, et passim.

37. Žižek, *On Belief,* 124.

38. See Luhmann, *Observations on Modernity,* 26, 58.

39. Hence too the rise of what might be described as the interactive compulsion, and, specifically, of media forms that simulate interaction in the form of readerly or audience participation—or, more properly, the mass observation of that interaction. And, it might be added, referred belief is at home in a culture saturated with deferred responsibility devices, from the answering machine (a machine for recording responses in one's absence) to psychoanalysis (the unconscious, or psychic apparatus, as a machine for recording absences in one's response—a pretty reliable storage medium of self-betrayal).

40. Poe, "Murders in the Rue Morgue," *Poetry and Tales,* ed. Patrick E. Quinn (New York, 1984), p. 398.

41. See Michel de Certeau, "What We Do When We Believe," *On Signs,* ed. Marshall Blonsky (Baltimore: Johns Hopkins University Press, 1985).

42. It would be possible to elaborate on the ties between the intensifications of modernist "observation" and modern imperatives of surveillance,

fictional and social. (On some of the relays between realist fiction and surveillance—in part localized in terms of everyday panopticisms, policing,
crime, and the "spy mania"—see my "Realism and the Fantasy of Surveillance," *Nineteenth-Century Fiction* 35, no. 4 [1981]: 506–534. See also
Christian Katti, "'Systematically' Observing Surveillance: Paradoxes of
Observation According to Niklas Luhmann's Systems Theory," in *CTRL
SPACE: Rhetorics of Surveillance from Bentham to Big Brother,* ed. Thomas
Y. Levin, Ursula Frohe, and Peter Weibel [Cambridge, MA: MIT Press,
2002], 50–63.) "Observation," in systems theory, is only incidentally, if
most melodramatically, visual ("to observe," in systems theory, is to "make
a distinction"). But on the manner in which this brokers a generalization
of the surveillance apriori and the techniques of observation in modernity,
see, for example, the closing passage of Luhmann's *Social Systems:* we "can
now encourage the owl of Minerva to stop hooting in the corner and begin
its flight into the night. We have instruments to watch over it, and we know
that its journey is a reconnaissance of modern society" (p. 488).

43. On the "erotic supersystem"—which relies on printed originals in matters
of love, which, in turn, makes that reliance suspect—see L. van der Weck-
Erlen, *Das goldene Buch der Liebe: Ein Eros-Kodex für beider Geschlechter*
(1907; Reinbek, 1978).

44. See Luhmann, *Love as Passion,* 236.

45. No doubt there are good disciplinary reasons for this. Doing otherwise
would be, for the historian, to cede the specificity of her field of expertness: the danger of history, and the social sciences more generally, merely
"becoming a branch of a more general interpretive, even literary activity."
Even literary! Not surprisingly, then, the conclusion drawn here is that "for
now the disciplines remain pretty much in their old places." This is not
least because of the methodologically concealed conservatism that governs
a good deal of "interdisciplinary," and "deconstructive," work. See *Beyond
the Cultural Turn: New Directions in the Study of Society and Culture,* ed.
Victoria E. Bonnell and Lynn Hunt (Berkeley: University of California
Press 1999), 4.

46. Bonnell and Hunt, *Beyond the Cultural Turn,* 11.

47. Bonnell and Hunt, *Beyond the Cultural Turn,* quoting Carolyn Walker
Bynum, 22.

48. For the editors of *Beyond the Cultural Turn,* the "ground" of the cultural
is the social, even as "the social" is, at least nominally, opened to some
groundbreaking. But this does not work if the ground of the cultural is
the social but the ground of the social is the social (the strict socialization of modern society). Hence one of the contributors to the collection,

the historian Karen Halttunen, notes in passing the centrality to modern conceptions of violence of the cultural turn: "Modern reading is the creation of a secluded inner realm of silent thought where individual selfhood can be generated, free from the pressures of the immediate presence of others" (*Murder Most Foul*, 82). This means that modern reading generates selfhood via the mass-mediated observation of others (here, via print). "Interiorization" thus means the preemptive "externalization" of the private and intimate in the generation of the private and intimate (intimacy as extimacy; as the half-believed commonplace now goes, the inside is the outside turned inside). But this registers only "in passing." For Halttunen, the modern "turn" involves a move from a prior direct and theological belief in evil to a gothic and mass-mediated and secular "noncomprehension" of evil. In effect, the turn from an external to a strictly social conception of evil means, for the social historian, that such conceptions "revolve in noncomprehension." This registers in miniature the manner in which, for the social historian, history without an extrahistorical ground (that is, a strictly historical conception of the historical) "revolves" in a groundless self-reflexivity. Along these lines, the historian forces her- or himself to run her or his own gauntlet—or, is forced to enact a legal self-exemption for her- or himself. Historicism is, of course, an historical concept. And reflexivity is not (to adapt Max Weber's way of expressing it) a streetcar that one can step off from at the next corner if one does not like where it is going. Along these lines, in the movement "beyond the cultural turn," the modernist self-reflexive turn is at once registered and bypassed. More exactly, a prior ground of direct belief is "angelized" through an appeal to a no-longer credible theological consensus. This "angelization" takes the form, even on the part of the most acute observers of the modernist turn, of a species of *no-longerism.* Thus, Peter Brooks, commenting on the rise of the melodramatic and gothic, holds that "melodrama starts from and expresses the anxiety brought by a frightening new world in which the traditional patterns of moral order no longer provide the necessary glue ... an anxious new world where the Sacred is no longer viable, yet rediscovery of the ethical imperatives that traditionally depended on it is vital." *The Melodramatic Imagination* (New York: Columbia University Press, 1984), 20, 19. And Eric Santner, commenting on Schreber's "modernity," concludes that "His 'secret history of modernity' suggests that we cross the threshold of that era where and when those symbolic resources no longer address the subject where he or she most profoundly 'lives,' which is, beginning at least with the European Enlightenment, the negative space hollowed out by the will to autonomy and self-reflexivity ... [The] community ... as a meaning-giving, symbolic whole can no longer … be experienced as fully trustworthy or of ultimate value" *My Own Private Germany* (Princeton: NJ: Princeton University Press, 1996), 145. It is not merely that this "where and when" remains spectral (among other observed self-observers, Hamlet? or Sade? or Schreber? 1600? Or 1800? Or 1900?). Nor is it merely that the gothic, for example, from the start, assails clichés to the point of the ludicrous, hence pathologizing self-reflexivity, from the start—and, we have seen, half-believing what it posits. The social conditions of that structure of half-belief is what I am tracking here. It would seem then that commentaries on the modernity of modernity repeat something like this referred "So have I heard and do in part believe." The systems theorist Luhmann offers his own version of no-longerism, in his observations on modernity: "To the extent that society imputes decisions and a corresponding mobility, there are no longer any dangers that are strictly externally attributable" (*Observations,* 71). The evolution and intensification of social contexts that exclude external attribution may thus provide one way of understanding the strict sociality of the cultural turn, and its modernity.

49. Cohen, *The Murder of Helen Jewett,* 3.

50. Lydia Huntley Sigourney, *Letters of Life* (New York, 1866), 39.

51. See Catherine Maria Sedgwick, *Means and Ends, or Self-Training* (New York, 1842), 27.

52. See *Serial Killers,* especially chapter 10, "Wound Culture: Trauma in the Pathological Public Sphere."

53. On some of the relays between true crime and true romance, with particular reference to the modern and contemporary American scene, see Sara L. Knox, *Murder: A Tale of Modern American Life* (Durham, NC: Duke University Press, 1998), 79–141.

54. See Patricia Crain, *The Story of A: The Alphabetization of America from* The New England Primer *to* The Scarlet Letter (Stanford, CA: Stanford University Press, 2000); Bernhard Siegert, *Relays: Literature as an Epoch of the Postal System,* trans. Kevin Repp (Stanford, CA: Stanford University Press, 1999); Luhmann, *Social Systems,* 302–303; and my "The Postal Unconscious," *Henry James Review* 21 (2000): 197–206.

55. See Siegert, *Relays;* and Jacques Derrida, *The Post Card: From Socrates to Freud and Beyond,* trans. Alan Bass (Chicago: University of Chicago Press, 1987). There is a complicated relation between deconstructive media studies and the style of recent German media studies that Friedrich Kittler centers (and to which Siegert's work contributes). But one difference between deconstructive and Kittlerian media studies is the difference, say, between the focus on *the postcard* and the focus on *the postal system.* That

is, in deconstructive media studies, the actual existence of particular media technologies in effect makes no difference, since any media technology (telephony, photography, the net, and so on) ultimately merely instances, or makes explicit, a writing-in-general always already, and in the beginning, in place (before the letter—and, so, before letters, i.e., the postal system). But this misses the problem, in that the problem is not at all "as if language and writing had not always existed, in order to prove that truth lies." The real point is (as Kittler puts it) that "the new" in the new media should "not be searched for in the realm of opinion and belief, of voluntary or unconscious deceptions," of identity options or performatives, etc.—not least in that the postal system and the epistolary novel have promoted such *liaisons dangereuses* for a long time, and not least given that social protocols of opinion, deception, and belief cannot be separated from the technical reality of the mass media. Rather, for Kittler, as for Luhmann (albeit with very different emphases: very different ways of taking up the materialities of communication), the new of the new media resides exactly—from the eighteenth-century "postal system" to the nineteenth-century "writing-down system" to the twentieth-century global computer-based network "operating system"—in the evolution of a reflexive, self-processing super-system that integrates all these systems. Or, as Kittler expresses it, it may be that the content of a medium is always another medium, but "the media of the past … did not also include their own meta-levels": a working model of autopoiesis, "networking begins and ends with pure self-referentiality." See Friedrich Kittler, "What's New about the New Media?" in *Mutations: Harvard Project on the City,* ed. Rem Koolhaas et al. (Barcelona: Actar Editorial, 2001), 58–69.

CHAPTER 4

Medium

Crime, Risk, Counterfactual Life

The Tremor of Forgery

New technologies are routinely experienced first in the idiom of pathology and violence: as crimes against humanity. Take the recent horror film *The Ring,* for example. There one finds a precise comparison of two rival ways of understanding the circuit of the mass media: the endless loop or transference of bodies and messages. On the first—which culminates in an apparent, but false, ending to the story—a serial violence via media operations (movie, videotape, television, telephone, and so forth) comes to an end when the murder of a child by her mother (that is, her proxy mother: nature is over) is exposed, the body found, and the undead put to rest. But things start up again immediately, and it turns out that the trauma and mourning thing is a cover for something else.

Hence, on the second "ending" of *The Ring,* the tape is not there to be decoded—analyzed, or psychoanalyzed—in order for an (always already known but repressed) mystery to be uncovered and things put to rights by working them through. The tape simply wants to be copied: the self-programming program wants to keep running. The real horror is that there may be nothing here deeper than that. And if it has to hang that on "topics" like trauma, ghosts, haunting, mourning, murder, regothicized trappings (deep wells, girls named Samarra, and the rest)—if it has to do that in order to seduce viewers to watch, to rewind, replay, and copy—so be it. The media, on this second view, do not mediate, they operate—and operate strictly to keep the operations going.

The gothic from the start—on the program of the supernatural explained, for example—rehearsed a self-generated and self-dispelled credulity (fiction stripped of fiction by fiction). In this way, it made clear what the strict socialization and secularization of society and the subject look like and feel like. It foregrounded its media apriori. And it previewed, too, that the horrors of ghosts, trauma, and torn bodies might well be preferable to the horror of a secular world and a strictly secular individuality that run on a loop—and for which the media (print to digital) is the unconscious of the unconscious. The modern rehearsals of the gothic (rings, white noise, the matrix, and also the regothicizations of deconstruction, contemporary traumatophilia, the wounded body as the return to the real, and so on) are, on this second view, small lessons in understanding media.

From spirit-tapping and telegraphy, to apparitions and photography, to auditory hallucinations and telephony, to the psychic detective and psychic television: there is a long history to this medium history. We know, that is, that there is a long history to a medium history that is also media history: to a communication with the past and the future via a successive series of psychotechnic machines.[1]

It does not take a popular TV crime show such as *Medium* to make this as literal as possible. That identification of the psychic apparatus and the communication apparatus appears at once as uncanny and as self-evident. Communicative history and the uncanny seem to indicate each other at every point, such that the double transparency of unconscious processes and media ones appears as something like the real uncanniness of the uncanny itself.[2]

There is no way of adjudicating between these two endings, these two accounts of the media apriori: since we can only communicate about communication in communication, there is no going behind this paradox. But, since it works anyway, behind our backs, that comes to look like a crime against humanity too.

Not least in the sequestered and over-coded world of the crime story. For one thing, these media protocols form and reform that world. The plot of Patricia Highsmith's crime novel *The Talented Mr. Ripley*, for instance, might simply be mapped by way of the movements of bodies and letters;

by the motions of persons, transport machines, media proxies, and messages; by the risk of their coincidence—for example, at the ubiquitous American Express offices (the outposts of globalization in Highsmith's world), where one exchanges identity papers for money and letters; and by the explosive violence of these doubles coming together.

Put simply, murder in Highsmith's Ripley novels, among many others, is where bodies and messages cross: where the distinction between body and message begins to tremble. Ripley's game is to replace persons (including himself) with letters, papers, voices, pictures, and personations. On this logic, murder and the media are not merely two ways of doing away with persons and bodies but two ways of saying the same thing (that is, two ways—as the military–media complex has it—of sending a message). Along these lines, the modern super-detective—the profiler—is at once noir technocrat and psychic medium. The point not to be missed is that the counterfactual reality of true and false crime is the precise register of its media apriori.

That media infrastructure makes for (to borrow a phrase from the crime fiction writer Patricia Highsmith) "the tremor of forgery" that runs through this counterfactual world, through a society self-experienced as a community of sheer contingency and danger, or potential danger. This is a mass-observed world of media doubling and double indemnity, of half-credences and statistical or technical premonitions, of unremitting and unremittingly calculated risk. In the next chapter of this book, I take up in a more extended way Highsmith's extraordinary versions of that media doubling of the world—and of the relays between murder and contingent modernity. Here I want to set out in a preliminary way what makes up what has come to be called the risk society, its media, and the style of crime proper to it.

Precrime

The basic premise of Philip K. Dick's short story (and now film) "Minority Report" is simple enough: in a more or less futuristic future, a system has been set up to stop crime by foreseeing it, "the Precrime system." The Precrime system works through "the prophylactic pre-detection of criminals through the ingenious use of mutant precogs [mutated humans], capable of previewing future events and transferring orally that data to analytic machinery." Hence "in their virtual function," the precogs are part of a system to make crime, centrally the crime of murder, literally unthinkable. "Potentially guilty individuals"—individuals whose crimes have been foreseen or previewed—are arrested and confined before they can do what they have been foreseen doing: that is, before they can commit the potential crimes for which they are prophylactically incarcerated.[3]

The real problem with the Precrime system is not exactly that it makes potential crime out to be the same as real crime: that is to say, that it simply arrests people for thought crimes. And this is not solely because the foreseen crimes are not merely thought but enacted in a potential future. It is because the matter of thought crime is itself a bit more complicated. The simple equation of thoughts of violence and acts of violence must of course be resisted: the thought or representation of murder is not equivalent to the act of murder. But the thought or representation of murder is by no means simply separate or apart from the act of murder: it is part of it. Murder without the thought of murder—premeditation, malice aforethought, and so on—is a different sort of act too. Thought is not the same as crime, but all crimes are thought crimes.

But the problem of precrime is yet deeper still. For if the intention (say, the intention to kill) is part of the act, the intention qualifies or constitutes the act *as* an act of murder—that is, as an act—which means that, under the preemptive Precrime system, one could in effect only do what one has not planned or decided to do. That makes doing less an act than an accident. But the difference between an act and accident is not as clear as it might at first seem. For if accidents happen, they do not *simply* happen. Rather, since, following Poe, "*accident* is admitted as part of the substructure," what qualifies as an act cannot be separated from the law of large numbers and a calculus of potential guilt. That is, even accidents are criminal acts under a statistical and probabilistic assessment, or auditing, of what might, or should, have been foreseen. Numbers determine substance.

To the extent that the legal system must assess the predisposition of the actor in assessing the nature of the criminal act, and to the extent that the ordinance of motives enters into the process, the nature of the act cannot be separated from the counterfactual, the virtual, and the probable "preview" of the crime.[4] The endless dilemma this entails is one reason for the emergence of the paradoxical category of the "motiveless crime" (or what Poe, in 1845 in his account of the criminal "imp of the perverse," called, more exactly, "motive not *motivirt*"). And this is one reason why the novel, and specifically the detective novel—from the start, the happy hunting ground of suspicion and motive—has progressively renounced inferences about motives.[5] Or, as a character in J. G. Ballard's recent novel *Cocaine Nights* concisely expresses it, "You won't find who was responsible by looking for motives. … [Here] like everywhere in the future, crimes have no motives. What you should look for is someone with no apparent motive for killing."[6]

Hence, if the Precrime system predetects *real* crimes through its *virtual* function, the problem is not that it confuses the real and the virtual. Instead, it makes visible a real virtuality—an ineradicable fictive or counterfactual component—in modern crime. Put simply, criminalization appears as a future effect or probable side-effect of what one does, or does not do. And what becomes a crime may be retroactively determined by its predictable effect or side-effects: by what one may do does. This is therefore not merely a matter of preobserving an act. It is a matter of observing the preobserving that constitutes the criminal act. Either way, crime cannot be separated from precognition, and precognition cannot be separated, in turn, from a calculus of probabilities and the auditing of potential futures.[7]

Another name for this real virtuality—for the future's effect on the present through a calculus of probability—is risk.[8] Consider, for example, the recent invention of something like a Precrime system: the computer software called CAPRisk. The CAPRisk system maps what can be described as "ulterior spaces":

> With the proliferation of commercial software [often adapted from military surveillance and data-processing technologies] and with the pervasiveness and growing sophistication of data collection, the realms over which computer simulations can operate are rapidly multiplying. The latest software in this genre is the CAPRisk

system, a crime analysis program developed by CAP Index. With CAPRisk, "any site can be scored for probability of crime occurrences"; retailers can therefore know how susceptible their proposed site will be to specific crimes, including homicide, rape, robbery, burglary, aggravated assault, larceny, and auto theft.

At present, seven of the nation's top ten retailers use CAPRisk services to indicate what security measures they should set up at particular locations or where to locate. The CAPRisk program maps commercially inhabitable spaces or, conversely, maps computer-generated no-man's-lands.[9]

This way of capitalizing on risk is familiar enough, not least in that the capitalization on risk is one way of understanding the ulterior motive of capitalism itself.[10] But here ulterior motives lose their latency or ulteriority. This system amounts to the mapping of *riskscapes:* to the mapping of social space as the potential scene of the crime.[11] It amounts, in the most general terms, to the proceduralization of uncertainty in the calculation of risk, and it amounts (it will be seen in a moment) to something like the criminalization of potentiality. By way of this mathematical, potential, and deferred reality—risks are not perceived or experienced directly (think of global warming; think of genetic time bombs)—the precognized future determines the present.

Now this version of real virtuality is familiar enough, too. After all, as risk theorists like to point out, every year a medium-size American city vanishes from the national scene, as it were, without a trace. And the car crash and its victims are perhaps only the most visible and most statistically proceduralized version of the new normality of the risk society: "risk is by now tolerated and normal in many areas of life."[12] As the great communicator of the culture of the normal accident J. G. Ballard expresses it, the car crash is "the pandemic cataclysm institutionalized in all industrial societies that kills hundreds of thousands of people each year and injures millions."[13]

This sort of vanishing, in contemporary novelist Chuck Palahniuk's terms, is "the opposite of a victimless crime."[14] What the "opposite of a victimless crime" means is, however, a bit paradoxical, in that the opposite of the victimless crime is not exactly a matter of victims without a crime. This is because the proliferation of victims without evidence of anything like a crime is something like the perfect crime. And one way of understanding the contemporary formation of a victim culture—the new victim order—is precisely on this model of the perfect crime. Or, as victim culture has also come to be called, "the world risk society."

This is the world of the "normal accident."[15] It is the world in which society as a whole comes to be understood, in the idiom of the insurance industry, as a global risk group. It is experience of everyday life in terms of the perpetual emergency state of generalized alert and unlocatable, uninsurable threat. It is the exposed world in which the gray zone between ordinary and terrorized life keeps expanding, such that it defines the "new normal."[16]

I want here to extend the investigation of true crime and mass belief by way of an anticipatory consideration of the exposed culture of the risk society. In the parts that follow, I do so centrally by way of the work of Patricia Highsmith, a novelist who maps that culture—this version of the pathological public sphere—in high relief. Here, if my examples come primarily from crime fiction, this is in part because it is fiction that schools individuals (that is, readers) in the counterfactual riskscapes of modernity. Fiction—and, not least, crime fiction—acclimatizes individuals to the protocols of reflexive modernity.

In modern crime writing and screening, true and false, a relentless reflexivity, intensified to the point of a pathological violence, enters into the interior of the criminal act. Highsmith's writings, for example, are not exactly crime fictions. They are, instead, novels in which crime and fiction—the counterfactual, the virtual, and the make-believe—indicate each other at every point. If "an individual in the modern sense is someone who can observe his or her own observing,"[17] the modern planners who are the modern killers in Highsmith's fiction are second-order observers, observers of observing, at the extreme. And, collaterally, in the intensity of their self-observation, they are something like seductive personalizations of the risk society at the extreme.

The abnormal normality of risk and the abnormal normality of an unremitting self-observation are bound up through and through in the makeup of these strange crimes, from the ordinance of motives that drives strangers on a train to Ripley's games of belief and make-believe. In her novel *A Suspension of Mercy* (originally titled *The Story-Teller*), a TV screenwriter is writing a novel called "*The Planners,* and it's about a group of people who decide to plan the experiences they want in life and live accordingly" (*Suspension*, p. 22).[18] The screenwriter himself keeps a journal in which he scripts the murder of his wife. A "free-lance inventor of fiction in private life," the "make-believe drama in which he had done away with her" (p. 155)—in the event of his wife's subsequent disappearance and violent death—takes on the look of precrime. Make-believe makes belief: "His pretending . . . only to himself, had suddenly become real" (pp. 125–126).

This reflexiveness at the level of the individual, and mandate to invent one's own bioscripts, to make oneself, is by now clear enough: it amounts to the "generalization of the principle of design and constructibility, which now encompasses even the subject whom it was once supposed to serve, exponentiates the risks."[19] It exponentiates the risks in part because the mandate for self-origination (the obligation to make oneself from oneself) is also, necessarily and paradoxically, a mandate for destruction and self-destruction. In the idiom of Palahniuk's *Fight Club,* "Maybe self-improvement isn't the answer. Tyler never knew his father. Maybe self-destruction is the answer."[20] In the idiom of Highsmith's screenwriter and self-scripter, this gives "a pleasant feeling of both creating something and of being a murderer. He would fill in the preceding pages" (*Suspension*, p. 83). The freedom, or cruelty, of self-instrumentalization extends to the very intimate practices of private life: "With the so-called second modernisation, the attitude that was hitherto reserved for the public as opposed to private life (reflexivity, the right to choose one's way of life instead of accepting it as imposed by tradition ['Tyler never knew his father'] has also penetrated the most intimate private sphere."[21] Or, in the idiom of the risk society, the social surges of individualization—by which the individual, like society, unremittingly becomes an issue and problem to itself—make freedom and the state of emergency two ways of saying the same thing: "We are all, or may be, always at risk."

This coupling of violence and feigning, or make-believe at the level of the individual, is bound up with something else. In Highsmith's novel *The Tremor of Forgery,* another writer transposes forged and factual experiences, until—amid the unremitting network of letters, papers, newspapers, and the "din of [radio] transistors" at the close—"even the typewriter [here the murder weapon itself] in his hand weighed nothing at all."[22] It is not merely that a ceaseless reflexivity—mass-mediated and mass-observed—enters into the interior of modern violence. That violence is self-observed and mass-observed through and through: that is, it refers back to the mass media, print and otherwise, at every point.

True crime, like true romance, is media-borne—and not least in that the technical protocols of that love and that violence are at once every-where self-evident in these scenes. The seductiveness of modern crime and of modern romance—the manner in which they seduce observers to observe violence and seduce observers to observe seduction—this seduction cannot be separated from its media protocols. At the same time, true crime and true romance—violence and sex and not least sexual violence—appear as just the opposite: as the direct and the real ("the Real") antidote to the media and mediation. Hence modern violence is the paramnesic symptom of the mass media: its image (it is everywhere) and its disavowal (it weighs nothing at all). The "tremor of forgery" ("the reality of the mass media") is along these lines at once generalized and pathologized.

I return to Highsmith in the chapters that follow and I can here merely anticipate how Highsmith's world works.[23] For now, we may note that Highsmith's killers, among many others, live in a self-observing world, a world of technically mediated "second thoughts." This is, I have been sug-gesting, also the self-observing territory of the risk society. Both the coun-terfactual reality of the risk society and this notion of second thoughts need a bit more unpacking. And it may be useful to set out in a little more detail what that society, and what the forms of thought, belief, and experi-ence that constitute it, look like.

Second Thoughts; or, "Is It Now?"

One of the paradoxes that make up the risk society is then the paradoxical situation of its members. On the one side, we know that "strictly speak-ing there is no such thing as an individual risk"; risk is a matter of the calculation of the normal or probable accident, the risk of becoming (in both the insurance and military sense) a casualty.[24] The notion of the casualty implies that injury or death is simply a by-product, or side-effect, of the normal order of things—that, on a long enough timeline, we are all, among other things, dead. On the other side, however, the stranded and endangered individual is the social unit of the risk society: the individual subject to the normal accident, subject to becoming a statistic, and subject to that endless drill of making oneself through decisions about what one wants and about what one wants to be. The social surges of individualization that mark, and in part define, modernity, are thus bound up through and through with protocols and reflexes of standardization. This amounts to the stranding of the nakedly individualized individual in the face of faceless threats, such as the law of large numbers. Hence "individualization ... means, in practical terms, learning to deal with paradoxical behavioral expectations. Individualization also means expanding the subjective room for freedom *and* complete market dependence, subjectivization *and* standardization of expression, increased self-reflexivity *and* overwhelming outside control."[25]

The modern calisthenics in self-making can thus operate by way of the by-now well-socialized internalization of these paradoxical imperatives called intuition. Or, on the way to that, it can operate via therapy or counseling or self-help books. Or it can operate via those self-help books about more or less self-helping individuals called novels.

Novels, like money, both individualize and standardize. Novels thus personalize these paradoxical conditions. And, to the extent that novels provide points of interest, identification, and seduction for the general reader—that is, characters—they invite him or her to do the same. Beyond that, to the extent that persons appear as personalizations of larger forces (as individualized correlates of the world), these larger forces are then experienced in reverse: as arrayed against persons. On this logic, the social imperative of self-making is turned around into the war of "self vs. society." Or, in its everyday or cold war version, the situation becomes one in which, unremittingly, "bureaucracies are criticized by self-help groups"[26]—groups that are of course in the process of bureaucratizing themselves.

This is, for example, the support group and wound culture world of Chuck Palahniuk's popular novel *Fight Club*. Here, it may be recalled, fight clubs are organized to confront the depersonalizing standardizations of self-help groups and a "space-monkey" consumerism: "You're one of those space monkeys. You do the little job you're trained to do. Pull a lever. Push a button. You don't understand any of it, and then you die" (*Fight Club*, p. 12). This is the world of what Palahniuk calls "single portion persons": the individuated individuals who fill plane seats, and whose seats, like their days, are numbered. It is the world of designer-"personalized" Ikea shopping. It is the world in which "home was a condominium on the fifteenth floor of a high-rise, a sort of filing cabinet for widows and young professionals. The marketing brochure promised a foot of concrete floor, ceiling, and wall between me and any adjacent stereo or turned-up television" (p. 41). It is a world, in short, made up of the "standardized collective existence of isolated and individuated mass hermits."[27]

And the fight clubs themselves, too, turn out to mass-produce space monkeys and their own bureaucracies—albeit a "Bureaucracy of Anarchy." The fight clubs themselves, that is, turn out to be "Support groups. Sort of" (*Fight Club*, p. 119), groups populated by lookalike space monkeys. In novels such as *Fight Club,* these familiar paradoxes in the normal operation of the risk society not merely lose their latency, such that they recall point by point what everyone already knows about that society. The novel is, beyond that, manifestly about recycling and "recall"—if not quite Philip K. Dick's nonplace of "total recall," in which "we can remember it for you wholesale."

For one thing, *Fight Club* exactly repeats the mathematical formula, the mathematical reality, of the risk society, in which (as Ulrich Beck summarizes it) risk means the calculus of probability: "risk = accident x probability."[28] In the idiom of *Fight Club*—the narrator works in the actuarial division of a car company, investigating crashes—the formula for calculating reality reads like this:[29]

Wherever I'm going, I'll be there to apply the formula. I'll keep the secret intact.

It's simple arithmetic.

It's a story problem.

If a new car built by my company leaves Chicago travelling west at 60 miles per hour, and the rear differential locks up, and the car crashes and burns with everyone trapped inside, does my company initiate a recall?

You take the population of vehicles in the field (*A*) and multiply it by the probable rate of failure (*B*), then multiply the result by the average cost of an out-of-court settlement (*C*).

A times *B* times *C* equals *X*. This is what it will cost if we don't initiate a recall.

If *X* is greater than the cost of a recall, we recall the cars and no one gets hurt.

If *X* is less than the cost of a recall, then we don't recall . . .

Consider this my job security. (pp. 30–31)

It is thus not merely that this "intact" secret is the open secret of the risk society—and the intact and open secret of that pyramid investment scheme called social security. The voice-over idiom of a schoolboy math problem—the generalized idiom of second-person narration that is the idiom of Palahniuk's fiction—is the voice of no one in particular talking to no one in particular. Reading Palahniuk is something like scanning the Internet for "information" and "how-to stuff" ("The three ways to make napalm: One, you can mix equal parts of gasoline and frozen orange juice concentrate. Two, you can mix ..." [*Fight Club*, p. 13]). It is, of course, all recycled stuff.

But the point not to be missed is that recycling and recall are the structural condition of the novel as well. It is not merely that the novel begins at the end, and works its way back (the "afterward" structure of crime fiction). The novel opens with a countdown to an explosion, the fight-club terrorist destruction of the world's tallest building: "We're down to our last ten minutes ... nine minutes ..." (*Fight Club*, p. 13). *Fight Club* thus previews the "unforeseen" event—September 11—endlessly foreseen in the popular novels and films of the preceding decade. The act is itself a reenactment ("the photo series of the Parker-Morris Building will go into all the history books … [t]he five-picture time-lapse series" [p. 14]. Hence the novel's final sentence: "We look forward to getting you back" (p. 208). The timescape of the risk society, like the millennial clocks that counted backward to the beginning of the millennium, is one in which the future affects and determines the present.

And one can, of course, recycle the notion of the risk society too as another instance of aborted critique. It makes perfect sense that the theorists of the risk society are hard-pressed to make a case for the very existence of something like a "risk society." The risk society, like the counterfactuals or real fictions that make it up, is a matter too of what Ulrich Beck evocatively calls "secondhand nonexperience."[30] And secondhand nonexperience looks like secondhand smoke and mirrors. Second-order observation and secondhand nonexperience mean that collective and individual action and thinking are of necessity a matter of talking about and dealing with unreal things: "Today we can speak of the future practically only in terms of the probable or improbable, that is, in terms of a fictively secured (duplicated by fictions) reality."[31]

This provides a way of redescribing the descriptions of co-optation or recycled rebellion that have, for example, governed debates about so-called postmodernism (attempts, for example, to distinguish between good [critical] and bad [complicit] postmodernisms—where the same examples inevitably show up on both sides of the ledger, and one last-resorts to ascriptions of "ambivalence," about which, one is, of course, resolutely ambivalent). In his history of the emergence of the modern state, *Critique and Crisis,* Reinhart Koselleck traces "the mutual polarisation of all eighteenth-century concepts," not least the concept of "critique," and "the critical function inherent in all dualisms."[32] The polarities that dominate early modern melodrama and the gothic, for example, represent something more than a simplified morality for the emergent mass reading public. The dualism encodes the basic polarity between moral and political orders; moral critique is in effect premised on its ineffectuality, on the absolute exclusion of the moral from the political order.

Something like that—radical critique self-immunized by the promise of its ineffectuality—continues to govern a range of "critical" postmodernism. It is necessary, however, to take this notion of critique a step further. Foreclosed rebellion—"We look forward to having you back"—means not just more of the same. It means something more than more of the same in that the reentry of observations about the social order into that order is one way of marking the reflexive order of modern society: society becomes reflexive, an issue and problem to itself, and the individual becomes reflexive, an issue and problem to himself.

It is not merely then that (as in the case of the recycling structure of *Fight Club*) it turns out that the solution is the problem. Like the code of dualisms that structures eighteenth-century concepts, the code of recall, recycling, or recidivism structures the contemporary concept of the risk society. And hence, "local" observations about baffled critique (or, as has become commonplace, critique reduced to a vague holding-out for the possibility of critique) miss the point. Solution-as-problem is one way of understanding the normal operation of the risk society, which is always putting itself at risk:

> The politics of fear lubricates the wheels of consumerism and helps to "keep the economy going" and steers away from the "bane of recession." Ever more resources are to be consumed in order to repair the gruesome effects of yesterday's resource consumption. Individual fears beefed up by the exposure of yesterday's risks are deployed in the service of collective production of the unknown risks of tomorrow.[33]

This was the more-of-the-same solution, the solution-as-the-problem solution, that tended to govern many even self-described "critical" responses to September 11th.

The counting back from the future to the present provides one measure of what it looks like to inhabit the counterfactual but no less real timescapes of the risk society. And it may provide one measure too, in the lurid staging of wound spectacles—support groups and fight clubs, for example—of the burgeoning sense of inhabiting a trauma culture today. The afterwardsness of trauma; its pathological reflexivity; the virtual effects of a wounding without a visible wound, and so on: all may be seen as something like a "personalization"—albeit in the idiom of pathology or violation—of that society. If the future affects the present above all in the form of risk, trauma provides the perfect individualization and psychologization of these social conditions—and a perverse acclimatization to them: the abnormal normality of trauma today looks like a retrofitting to the new normal. And to the extent that risk is at once counterfactual and real, such that "what escapes perceptibility no longer coincides with the unreal,"[34] the necessarily phantasmatic dimension of trauma, its retroactivity, and its real virtuality provide a perfect measure too of what experience comes to look like in the risk society: that is, secondhand nonexperience.

Here we might consider Haruki Murakami's recent novel about foreclosed futures and real virtuality *Hard-Boiled Wonderland and the End of the World,* which opens with this paragraph:

> The elevator continued its impossibly slow ascent. Or at least I imagined it was ascent. There was no telling for sure: it was so slow that all sense of direction simply vanished. It could have been going down for all I knew, or maybe it wasn't moving at all. But let's just assume it was going up. Merely a guess. Maybe I'd gone up twelve stories, then down three. Maybe I'd circled the globe. How would I know?[35]

It is not hard to see that the elevator in this opening is a scale model of the world: "this elevator was so spacious it could have served as an office. Put in a desk, add in a cabinet and a locker, throw in a kitchenette. ... You might even squeeze in three camels and a midrange palm tree while you were at it" (*Hard-Boiled,* pp. 1–2). Or, rather, this "space" is part of a world that proliferates scale models, theme-park replicas, of itself.

These are scale models of the "sequestration" of society and of experience. The experience of still bodies in moving machines is perhaps the defining experience of machine culture (if, as Hobbes expressed it, "life itself is but motion," the transfer of motion from body to machine is also the transfer of stilled life to the machine process). Or, as Murakami puts it, "Stationary in unending silence, a still life: *Man in Elevator*," (*Hard-Boiled*, p. 2). But to call this "experience" is a bit misleading. After all, one has no more direct experience of the space's movement than one has direct experience that the globe is round and thus something that can be circled. One has only referred experience of both—the sort of experience one is told about, or receives through the mass media, or reads about in novels.

The space is, beyond that, a life-support system, but a system that seems to suspend both life ("antiseptic as a brand-new coffin") and support ("all of which made me feel utterly defenseless"). In this "highly exceptional reality" stripped of all controls that can be operated from within and of all sense of control operated from without, the narrator can do little more than whistle "Danny Boy" and kill time by practicing calculations by which his right hand does not know what his left hand is doing. So much for firsthand experience! The automatically opening door connects to "a long corridor": "We were walking around and around, like in an Escher print ... not a window in sight" (*Hard-Boiled*, p. 10). That is, the narrator enters into the real virtual world of *Korridorbildung* ("the formation of corridors") space, the modernist space (as Carl Schmitt defined it) of evolving self-sufficient bureaucratic systems, systems materialized in offices, lobbies, antechambers, secretarial pools, and auditing domains, such that the movement of bodies and information indicate each other at every point, and "print" and "space" translate each other at every point.[36]

The corridor-formation world is also the world of Dick's "Minority Report," not merely in its tracking of the materialities of communication (for example, "They had come to a descent lift ... the lift left them out. ... Doors opened and closed, and they were in the analytical wing" ["Minority Report," pp. 2–3]) but also in its tracking of conditions of belief and disbelief, of reflection and secondhand nonexperience, in the futures market in crime. The story provides something like a keyword index of the risk society ("Risk? Chance? Uncertainty? With precogs around?" [p. 25]). The story, that is, italicizes by repetition the half-credences or half-beliefs that are the collective state of belief in the risk society. It is not merely that the world of "Minority Report" is, on all counts, a programmatically self-observed world. Beyond that, the self-observations of the act, the proleptic reports on it, enter into the act ("As soon as precognitive information is obtained, *it cancels itself out.* ... Faced with the knowledge of the first report, I had decided *not* to kill Kaplan. That produced report two. But faced with *that* report, I changed my mind back" [p. 42]. And so on.) The reentry of observations about the working of the system into the system is something like a key index of systems theory and second-order observation, too. True crime thus cannot be separated from talk about unreal things, the counterfactuals that make up secondhand nonexperience—from the tremor of forgery. "Minority Report" begins in this way: "The first thought Anderton had when he saw the young man was: *I'm getting bald. Bald and fat and old.* But he didn't say it aloud. Instead, he pushed back his chair, got to his feet, and came resolutely around the side of his desk" (p. 1).

Anderton's first thought is thus a series of second thoughts, the second thoughts by which the precognized or potential future affects the present, positing interiorities, latencies, motives, and resolutions—positing individuality—along the way. If then the modern individual is someone who can reflect on his or her own reflection, then the uncertain region of second thoughts is the place proper to the individual now. And if periodizing individuality in this way looks like a way of outdating the very notion of the individual, then one might simply, or incredulously, ask along with the nymph-like precog of Spielberg's film version of "Minority Report," "Is it *now?*"

Notes

1. See, for example: Friedrich Kittler, *Gramophone, Film, Typewriter,* trans. Geoffrey Winthrop-Young and Michael Wutz (Stanford, CA: Stanford University Press, 1999); *New Media, 1740–1915,* ed. Lisa Gitelman and Geoffrey B. Pingee (Cambridge, MA: MIT Press, 2003); Avital Ronell, *The Telephone Book: Technology, Schizophrenia, Electric Speech* (Lincoln: University of Nebraska Press, 1989); Jeffrey Sconce, *Haunted Media: Electronic Presence from Telegraphy to Television* (Durham, NC: Duke University Press, 2000); Stefan Andriopoulos, "Psychic Television," *Critical Inquiry* 31 (Spring 2005): 618–637.

2. One might call this "techno-gothic" if it were not the case that the gothic is involved with the technical media from the start. Static on the telephone line, for Bell and Watson, signaled spirit communication; and, later, static

on the screen, white noise, looked like ghosts. In films like *Ringu* or its remake *The Ring,* it still does—albeit with a well-rehearsed knowingness that, again, does not stop not knowing that.

3. Philip K. Dick, *Minority Report* (London: Gollancz, 2002), 19.

4. See my *Serial Killers: Death and Life in America's Wound Culture* (New York: Routledge, 1998), 4–5, 187–188.

5. See, for example, Niklas Luhmann, *Observations on Modernity,* trans. William Whobrey (Stanford, CA: Stanford University Press, 1998), 19; and Niklas Luhmann, *Social Systems,* trans. John Bednarz Jr. with Dirk Baecker (Stanford, CA: Stanford University Press, 1995), xliii.

6. J. G. Ballard, *Cocaine Nights* (London: Flamingo, 1996), 182.

7. These looped temporalities are, of course, basic presumptions of the cybernetic turn. As Norbert Wiener observes, with reference to the design of antiaircraft guidance systems (which gave rise to real-time computational systems generally), the task was "to shoot the missile, not at the target, but in such a way that missile and target may come together in space at some time in the future … to predict the future of a curve … is to carry out a certain operation on its past." See Norbert Wiener, *Cybernetics: Or, Control and Communication in the Animal and the Machine* (Cambridge, MA: MIT Press, 1965), 5. The concern today with "pure potentialities" (with the unpredicability of "a future yet to come")—for instance, in the work of Derrida and Agamben—has been one way of parrying this cybernetic temporality (and in part a way of disavowing the direct indebtedness to cybernetics of deconstruction and Lacanian psychoanalysis both—an indebtedness explicit, for example, in Derrida's *Grammatology* and throughout Lacan's work). That is, a simple opposition of probability and potentiality will not take us very far here: contingency is the defining attribute of modernity, not its antidote.

8. Cf. Luhmann, *Social Systems,* xlii: "the future affects the present above all in the form of risk."

9. Sze Tsung Leong, "Ulterior Spaces," in *Project on the City 2: Harvard Design School Guide to Shopping,* ed. Chihua Judy Chung et al. (Cologne: Taschen, 2001), 765–812; Susan Reda, "Crime Risk Predictions Aid Store Site Selection," *Stores* (September 1997): 39.

10. See, for example, Michael Rustin, "Reinterpreting Risk," in *Schools of Thought: Twenty-Five Years of Interpretive Social Science,* ed. Joan Scott and Debra Keates (Princeton, NJ: Princeton University Press, 2001), 349–363; and Niklas Luhmann, *Risk: A Sociological Theory,* trans. Rhodes Barrett (New York: A. de Gruyter, 1993).

11. On the notion of the "riskscape," see Susan Cutter, quoted in Cynthia Deitering, "The Postnatural Novel," in *The Ecocriticism Reader,* ed. Cheryll Glotfelty and Harold Fromm (Athens: University of Georgia Press, 1996), 200; and Ursula K. Heise, "Toxins, Drugs, and Global Systems: Risk and Narrative in the Contemporary Novel," *American Literature* 74, no. 4 (December 2002): 747–778.

12. See Ulrich Beck, *Risk Society: Towards a New Modernity,* trans. Mark Ritter (Sage: London, 1992), 46.

13. J. G. Ballard, *Crash* (New York: Vintage, 1985), 6.

14. Chuck Palahniuk, *Survivor* (New York: Anchor Books, 1999).

15. See Charles Perrow, *Normal Accidents: Living with High-Risk Technologies* (Princeton, NJ: Princeton University Press, 1999).

16. The central references here are: Beck, *Risk Society*; Beck, *World Risk Society* (Malden, MA: Polity Press, 1999); and Luhmann, *Risk*. See also, for example: *Risk, Environment and Modernity: Towards a New Ecology,* ed. Scott Lash et al. (London: Sage, 1996).

17. Luhmann, *Observations on Modernity,* 7.

18. Patricia Highsmith, *A Suspension of Mercy* (1965; New York: Norton, 2001). Subsequent references in text abbreviated as *Suspension.*

19. Beck, *Risk Society,* 200.

20. Chuck Palahniuk, *Fight Club* (New York: Henry Holt, 1996), 49.

21. Slavoj Žižek, "Kant with (or against) Sade?" in "The Ethics of Violence," special issue, *New Formations* 35 (Autumn 1998): 106.

22. Patricia Highsmith, *The Tremor of Forgery* (New York: Atlantic Monthly Press, 1969), 248.

23. See chapter 5, "Vicarious Crime" and chapter 7, "Postscript on the Violence–Media Complex (and Other Games).

24. Francois Ewald, "Insurance and Risk," in *The Foucault Effect: Studies in Governmentality,* ed. Graham Burchell, Colin Gordon, and Peter Miller (Chicago: University of Chicago Press, 1991), 202–203.

25. Helmuth Berking, cited in Luhmann, *Observations,* 102–103.

26. Beck, *Risk Society,* 33.

27. Beck, *Risk Society,* 132.

28. Beck, *World Risk Society,* 137.

29. Compare here James M. Cain's *Double Indemnity*—a novel premised on the statistical doubling of the world (a world defined by double-entry or "multiple-card bookkeeping" (1936; London: Orion, 2002, 37)—and a narrative doubled in writing and dictaphone recording both. Compare too Patricia Highsmith's *Ripley's Game* (1974; London: Vintage, 1999), in which the crime world is nothing but the playing out of such a thought

problem, exercise, or game: "Tom thought. That was a nice Gallic touch of detection, the four minutes, like a problem in arithmetic for children also, Tom thought. If a train is going at one hundred kilometres per hour, and one Mafioso is tossed out, and a second Mafioso is found tossed out six and two-thirds of a kilometre distant from the first Mafioso, how much time has elapsed between the tossing out of each Mafioso? Answer: four minutes" (p. 123). On *Ripley's Game* and the crime system as game, see chapter 7, "Postscript on the Violence–Media Complex (and Other Games)."

30. Beck, *Risk Society,* 71.
31. Luhmann, *Observations,* 95.
32. Reinhart Koselleck, *Critique and Crisis: Enlightenment and the Pathogenesis of Modern Society* (Cambridge, MA: MIT Press, 1988), 102, 116.
33. Zigmunt Bauman, "The Solution as Problem," *The Times Higher Education Supplement* 13 (November 1992): 25.
34. Beck, *Risk Society,* 44.
35. Haruki Murakami, *Hard-Boiled Wonderland and the End of the World,* trans. Alfred Birnbaum (New York: Vintage, 1993), 1. Subsequent references in text abbreviated as *Hard-Boiled.*
36. See Carl Schmitt, *Gespräch über die Macht und den Zugang zum Machthaber* (Pfullingen, 1954).

CHAPTER 5

Vicarious Crime

Vicarious Life

It is not difficult to see that Patricia Highsmith's crime novels are drawn to the problem of belief, or half belief: to the problem of making oneself and others believe. After all, her most popular killer—and for a time something of an alterego—carried the name of this problem: "Believe it or not, old believe-it-or-not Ripley's trying to put himself to work."[1] What is perhaps less evident is how both crime and belief, in Highsmith's fiction, are bound up through and through with the reality of the mass media: with, for example, reality shows like *Ripley's Believe It or Not!*

If this is less than evident, it is by no means because the mass media in the most general sense—the modern technological media of body transport and message transport like the postal system, movies, trains, planes, telephones, dictaphones, newspapers, radio, television, or (still) novels—are "missing" from Highsmith's novels. They are everywhere. At the "Ripleylike" (*Ripley*, p. 177) moment just glanced at, for example, Tom is talking on the telephone, about to go to American Express to get his mail, before boarding a plane, identity papers in hand, in a novel. The mass media are everywhere in Highsmith, universalized and therefore banalized, even trivialized. The media are, it seems—like the purloined letter of Poe's postal system mystery—a bit too self-evident to be seen. Or, better, in that a mass-mediated world is a self-observing world, the universalization of the media (the media apriori) is one way in which this observation may remain unobserved—and one way in which this nonobservation may itself become visible.

Put simply, the mass media make up the background reality of this world: "A cool chill ran down Chester. This was fact. It had been on the radio. Thousands of people had heard it. 'It'll certainly be in the papers today, though.'"[2] The mass media perform this function because (in the modern world, to the extent to which it is modern) nothing else can perform this function: the function of indicating what is known and what is known to be known about.[3] It makes up public reality: that is, what the public—people like you and me—know, and who, knowing that and reflecting on it, reflexively make up a public.

But if the mass media make up the background reality of this world, it thus seems a made-up—a selected, framed, and therefore suspect—world. To say "this was fact" is to reflect on factuality and thus in part to discredit it. After all, the very dailiness of the news makes it suspect—or it is just fantastic luck that, for example, once the networks, some time ago, moved from 15 minutes to a half hour of evening news, there has been exactly one half hour of news to report every day.[4]

In the nature of the news as news, that is, the reporting on the event becomes the event reported on. (And this always "Now more than ever!"[5]) This is not a construction of the mass media in the sense of a distortion to be sorted out and cast out (although there are of course lots of distortions and lots of things to be cast out). It is the "constructedness" of the mass media as *a necessary selection and framing of what it observes* (it cannot show everything) and *observation of what, and how, it frames and selects* (it must show, in the interest of the reality it makes reference to, that it cannot).

This is no doubt one of the ways in which modern society makes visible and opens itself to its self-conditioning. The media, that is, generate their own plausibility themselves. And if the media are reflected in themselves, if they rehearse within themselves this game of deception and realization, this means that the mass media necessarily treat this self-conditioning itself, in turn, as an event.[6] This is social reflexivity at its purest. And the characters in Highsmith's fiction endure this unremitting reflexivity like the weather: "He had had what he considered a good day."[7] Hence, even the weather must be reported: "*You* look like it's raining outside" (*Found,*

p. 46). There is no getting "back" of this background—and therefore no doing away with the solicitation to do just that: "The registration and revelation of reality make a difference to reality. It becomes a different reality, consisting of itself plus its registration and revelation."[8] And so on. A reading world, a mass-media world, we have seen, is a self-observing world.[9]

But such equations read from right to left as well as from left to right: a self-observing world (a world that observes and observes its observing) is a mass-reading and, now, mass-viewing, world. Whatever "democracy" may be, for instance, and whatever "the public" may be, for instance, we know that they are "supported by the mechanical processing of anonymous discourses."[10] That is to say, print and the public, and publicness and the mass media today, support, and expose, each other at every point. This indicates the manner in which the mass media effect and communicate the social tie—and thus makes possible *vicarious life,* in contemporary culture. It indicates also, then, how the mass media cannot cease half-exposing the social tie as nothing but an effect of communication.

These special effects of the mass media provide one way of understanding the intensifications of reflexivity in contemporary culture and the forms of referred belief it supports. The novel, for example, from the mid-nineteenth century on, progressively yields up its monopoly on stories of love and crime to a rivalry among media forms. The stories the novel continues to tell, in turn, turn out to be stories of vicarious life and death: that is, a vicarious life and death sponsored by, or yielded up to, the double reality of the mass media.

This intensification of reflexivity is nowhere clearer than in the strange narrative disposition that is Highsmith's signature style of narration. The strangeness of this narrative way of seeing can, for the moment, be less explained than exemplified. It is a form of showing and telling that only makes sense if one takes seriously the situation of the novel among the mass media and if one takes seriously the manner in which the media make up our situation.

Highsmith's fiction registers this competition on the formal and not merely topical level. Here is, for example, the opening paragraph of *The Talented Mr. Ripley:*

Tom glanced behind him and saw the man coming out of the Green Cage, heading his way. Tom walked faster. There was no doubt that the man was after him. Tom had noticed him five minutes ago, eyeing him carefully from a table, as if he weren't *quite* sure, but almost. He had looked sure enough for Tom to down his drink in a hurry, pay and get out. (*Ripley,* p. 5)

In the Ripley novels, sentence after sentence begins with "Tom." This is, in part, a delimitation to Tom Ripley's point of view. It is, in part, a way of viewing Tom's view of his point of view. But such descriptions are a bit misleading. In this narrative observation of the self-observed observer, a doubling takes place. In effect, "Tom" reads as "I"; but if "Tom" reads as "I," then "I" reads as "Tom's" double. The effect, that is, is something like that of a first-person speaker speaking of himself and seeing himself in the third person. This is something like an intensification, or italicization, of represented discourse—or better, an indication of the social and personal conditions of identity and relation that the "spreading" of represented discourse in modern writing indexes and rehearses.

Highsmith, in *Plotting and Writing Suspense Fiction,* describes the "plague" of "the first-person singular" as a narrative point of view. As she expresses it, "I don't know what was the matter, except that I got sick and tired of writing the pronoun 'I,' and I was plagued with an idiotic feeling that the person telling the story was sitting at a desk writing it. Fatal!" But the solution to this problem is not an abandonment of the first-person singular but its paradoxicalization. She defines this solution with an astonishing directness, and exactly in terms of the paradox of self-reflexivity at the level of the subject: "I prefer the point of view of the main character, written in the third-person singular."[11]

This is, of course, nothing but the talented Mr. Ripley's talent: the talent, or compulsion, of impersonation and self-impersonation via oral and written and visual media of communication. That singular talent might more simply be called, not impersonation, but *personation.* Ripley (like a range of other fictional and real-life serial killers) lives in the third-person singular.[12]

The point here is not to reduce such instances to a (self-evident) aesthetic or individual self-consciousness. It is necessary instead to shift the point of vantage—a slight shift, perhaps, but one with large consequences. It is necessary to take seriously how the recursive autonomy of art prepares the ground, as it were, for the paradoxical social structure of reflexive modernity, how the first operates as dress rehearsal for the second.

Highsmith's narrative way of seeing, in short, lends to self-observation the look of omniscience and to the counterfactual the feel of objective description. If the modern individual is the individual who can observe his or her own observation, then one may rediscover here a modernized version of the romantic conception of the double: "Nobody can know himself, unless he is both himself and an other."[13]

But this is somewhat misleading too. The proliferation of doubles and doubling in Highsmith's crime writing has a different logic than that of the Romantic double. It is bound directly to the forms of life sponsored by the mass media. The exact model for the doubling of reality and producing of doubles that mark Highsmith's crime writing is not hard to find. That model (it will be seen) is the cinema. I am referring in part to the mechanized doubling of act and observation that the cinema posits as its condition and as its mode of operation. That mechanized doubling of observation and act *reenters* as the film's subject or topic, from the earliest instances of film to the present. Highsmith's novels are everywhere shot through by *the psychotechnologies of everyday life*—above all, by modern motion industries like trains, the postal service, and the movies.

These motion industries, and their relations to modern crime, remain to be elaborated. For now, it may be seen that, in the doubled reality of the mass media, reflexivity is generalized as a social and not merely a personal or psychological state. It is the general condition of an unremitting social self-reflexivity. This makes for an endless and violent paradox: the strict socialization and sequestration of the social order (a social order that makes itself from itself) requires the strictly autopoietic and autonomous individual (who makes himself from himself). But since the first mandates, and thus aborts, the second, the autopoietic autonomy "borrowed" from art opens the possibility of unremitting violence, and enters directly into the story of modern criminality.

The enduring of reflexivity and autonomy is both the talent and the sentence of Highsmith's killers and artists (who are, for that reason, often the same person). There is nothing "deeper" than the merely general reader's observing how a character observes, and how he observes or fails to observe that. As a character in *The Suspension of Mercy* expresses it: "everything was a matter of attitudes … the attitude had been caused by his attitude."[14] As another observer puts it, in *The Cry of the Owl:* "I have the definite feeling if everybody in the world didn't keep watching to see what everybody else did, we'd all go berserk."[15] Or, as another puts it, even more succinctly, in *Those Who Walk Away:* "Perhaps identity, like hell, was merely other people."[16]

This is, crucially, a narrative observation that presupposes a mass audience—a viewing or listening public—as the ulterior or "third person" in this world. And, along these lines, the media apriori enters into the interior of modern crime. For that reason, self-examination or self-disclosure, for example, in Highsmith's fiction takes the form of its media equivalent: the interview ("If he were interviewed, he would say, '[Murder] was terrific! There's nothing in the world like it'").[17] Introspection is a media event, and interior states look like self-interviews—albeit not very revealing ones. Talking, for example, is not merely observing one's own speech act at a distance, telephonically ("For a moment he heard his own voice saying …"). It is like listening to a recording ("like a phonograph playing his head" [*Ripley,* p. 218]), or it is like making one ("as if he talked to an inanimate thing like a dictaphone" [*Strangers,* p. 250]).

The mistake would be to understand this becoming visible and general of communication media in the situation of private and public relations as a fall into unreality—the invasion of a "plague of fantasies" into real life (Žižek), or a version of what has been called "the perfect crime," the murder of reality, without a trace (Baudrillard). It will be recalled that the phrase "real life" comes from a novel. The distinction between real and fictional reality is made from inside fiction; it is part of the narratively produced believability of the unbelievable.

Here we might consider the paradoxical economy of two related truth-seeking modern fictional genres. The first is the Enlightenment genre of "the supernatural explained." The second is the more recent genre of crime writing, what might be called "the mystery revealed."

In the fictional genre of the supernatural explained, ghosts, for example, may be introduced into the story in such a way as to acquire temporary plausibility, or half-credence. This can then be revoked, in the interests of an enlightened truth that excludes superstitious fiction. But, of course, the implausible is revoked precisely as a demonstration of the consistency of a larger narrative plausibility. The test of reality, the distinction between what can be treated as reality and what cannot be (the fictional) is thus made internal to the fictional system. Fiction is lifted out of fiction by fiction.[18]

This version of fictional reality, or self-induced plausibility, can be made a bit clearer by glancing at the classic form of the crime story, "the mystery revealed." Here the initial eruption of crime is taken to disrupt a normative social order, an order that is then restored when the mystery is revealed, "mere" stories (lies) exposed, and the crime solved. Fictional stories yield to the true story. But here too the distinction between truth and fiction can only be made from within fiction: that is, in the interests of the plausibility of a narrative system that must exclude, for example, rabbit-out-of-a-hat solutions as a violation of the consistency of that system.

The exclusion of such "trick" solutions is, crucially, an exclusion of a deus-ex-machina break in the order of things.[19] And the exclusion of such miracles is thus the exclusion of an inconsistency in the real—that is to say, in an utterly socialized and utterly secularized order of things. It marks the installation of the basic fantasy—the coherence of the social system, as the real order of things—via the deconstruction of a self-generated uncertainty. The crime system and the social system thus include each other.[20]

This is one reason why crime, true and false, has become a strange attractor in the pathological public sphere. Here I want to forward these matters of referred observation and belief, vicarious life and the reality of the mass media, centrally by way of Highsmith's inaugural crime novel, *Strangers on a Train*. But first it is necessary to put in place one final, and central, element in the nexus of vicarious life and its media apriori: *vicarious crime*.

I take the notion of vicarious crime from the nineteenth-century legal historian Savigny, in his account of "juristical persons" under the law. It may be worth setting out Savigny's account in some detail, not exactly for the notion of legal persons he summarizes (the notion by now may be familiar enough) but instead for the biotechnologies that account makes visible, biotechnologies that bind modern sociality and modern crime.[21]

The juristical person, as a legal subject, is, it will be recalled, not the natural subject or individual man (not one "who carries his claim to Jural Capacity in his corporeal appearance": that is, has a body). He is, rather, an "artificial subject admitted by means of a pure fiction."[22] Juristical persons "represent" the place of persons, and represent that place only as "feigned persons" or "mere fictions."[23]

This feigning or fiction reaches its limit with respect to the matter of will. The limited capacities of such a feigned person—in short, the capacity to hold or to transfer property—are "imputed to it, in consequence of a Fiction, as its own Will." But this is not to be confused with a "power of thinking and willing" on the part of this artificial subject. The juristical person is a pure fiction; one might speak of the "injured Personality" of the juristical person but can scarcely make this out to be a matter of "injured Feelings."[24] One could no more look "back" of that fiction for the feelings or will that have not been imputed to it or made part of it than one might look back of a picture to see its backside.[25]

Now the distinction between real and feigned persons is not hard to undo. But it holds something else in place: the subject of modern crime. "The Criminal Law," Savigny argues, "has to do with the Natural Man, as a thinking, willing, sensible Being." The crucial point is that the "Juristical Person, however, is nothing of this sort, but simply a Being having Property, and lies therefore completely outside the reach of the Criminal Law." Hence, a juristical person "cannot *commit* a crime": he is not made that way. What looks like an offense committed by a feigned person "is, in reality, always that of its members or of its Representative, and therefore, of Individual Men or of Natural Persons."[26]

The juristical person is thus something like "madmen and minors" under the law. They resemble persons but are "destitute of the Natural Capacity of Action"—and hence of the will to offend—"for which reason an artificial Will is procured for them in the person of a Representative" or guardian. But it would make as little sense to punish the minor or madman for the offense of his guardian as it would be to impute crime (or the will to commit it, which qualifies the criminal act as criminal and as an act) to a made up person. "In such a case," Savigny concludes, "no one has ventured to assert the possibility of *a vicarious Crime*."[27]

A good deal is at stake here. For one thing, the possibility of vicarious crime is fundamental to, among other things, fundamentalism: to a conception of the world that includes the logic and transmission of original sin ("In Adam's Fall, We Sinned All") and the possibility of its reparation by proxy. Hence the turn from a religious to a strictly secular conception of crime could not be more clearly marked. It is not hard to see that this secular or social turn remains bound then to deep uncertainties about crime and will. Modern maladies of the will are also crises in criminal law, such that, for example, the sociality and the self-sovereignty of the individual, popular sociology and popular psychology, come apart (or appear as each other's blind spot).[28] It means that modern crime and modern sociality form two sides of the same formation. And it means that reflexive modernity and its media apriori make up the realities of vicarious life and vicarious crime both.

Hence the formation of a pathological public sphere, centered on traumatic violence and violent crime, as the model of shared and collective life. Hence too the strange attraction between crime and the vicarious reality of the mass media. If vicarious crime, in a religious world, meant that God held the world together by ceaselessly observing it, that function today is held by the mass media, whose providence is the doubled reality of second-order observation.

If being-in-print was the relay point of private and public life in the writing-down network of print culture, being-in-the-media is the relay system of intimacy and publicness today. Modern crime cannot be separated from the reality of the mass media, which enters into its interior. The mass media in turn reflexively return to the scene of the crime as the return to the real. Vicarious life—the possibility or credibility of the social tie—and vicarious crime solicit each other. Crime fiction is then, at the least, a good way of testing out modern distinctions between real and fictional persons and real and fictional reality. And Patricia Highsmith's murder and media story *Strangers on a Train* may be a good way of mapping them in that vicarious life and vicarious crime form its subject.

Media Doubling

There is an extraordinary scene at the close of Highsmith's first novel, *Strangers on a Train* (1949), a scene that draws into relation a dense cluster of these concerns. These are concerns, at bottom, about modern crime, its psychology, its sociality, its media, and its modernity.

The scene takes place in a hotel room, where Guy Haines has arranged a face-to-face meeting with his murdered wife's lover, Owen Markman. He wants to explain, or to confess, his part in that murder. He wants, in effect, to explain the plot of the novel, which is about strangers and trains:

> You see, I met Charles Bruno on a train, coming down to Metcalf … I told him [my wife] Miriam's name. I told him I hated her. Bruno had an idea for a murder. A double murder. … My mistake was in telling a stranger my private business. … Bruno's idea was that we should kill for each other, that he should kill Miriam and I should kill his father. … The whole idea rested on the fact that there was no reason for the murders. No personal motives. (*Strangers,* p. 246)

Strangers on a Train thus not only takes on the possibility of vicarious crime: vicarious crime is the very premise and plot of the novel. Two strangers meet on a train and exchange motives and murders. This is, in short, a novel about "double murder" and about "double-track minds." That doubling involves something more than the transferences of guilt, motive, identity, and act that put the novel into motion. It involves something more than that because the transference, or doubling, of guilt, identity, and act is itself the motive—the "no-motivation scheme"—for crime.

Doubles proliferate in Highsmith's fiction. But they are only superficially versions of the romantic doppelgänger, ghosts of self-reflection. (That is, what happens when readers, who have always already been taken in by words, confuse their lives with their reading, and hallucinate print into characters like themselves.[29]) Doubling in Highsmith is the register of a reflexivity (social and individual) gone wild. That reflexivity is, in turn, inseparable from the media and mass-transport technologies that double reality and produce doubles—for example, the strangers on trains, dressed alike, reading the same papers, sharing the same daily commute and the same daily communications, and so on.

The face-to-face confession that ends the novel, for instance, is neither quite face-to-face nor quite a confession. Interaction and reflexive speculation are turned over to machines. The sequencing of this turnover could not be more clearly marked. Just prior to this scene, Guy has written a long confession and what is most visible here is the sheer materiality of writing and posting:

> He looked at the big sleek-surfaced sheets of drawing paper. ... Then he sat down and began to write from the upper left-hand corner across. ... His writing blackened three of the big sheets. He folded the sheets, put them into an oversized envelope, and sealed it. For a long while he stared at the envelope ... wondering at its separateness now from himself. ... This was for Anne. Anne would touch this envelope. Her hands would hold the sheets of paper and her eyes would read every word. (*Strangers*, pp. 240–241)

Writing and printing develop possibilities of social communication without (physical or spatial) interaction.[30] But letter-writing here hesitates the potential separation between message and bodies, holding to the physicality of the letter and hallucinating the body of the receiver/reader, her eye and hand and touch.

The plan to contact Markman in person—body transport matching message transport in this case—tacitly points to the physicality of letters too. It comes to Guy's mind only with this writing: "The name had swum into his mind mechanically. He hadn't thought of Owen at all until he wrote the letter. ... If he owed it to anyone he owed it to Markman" (*Strangers*, pp. 242–243). Owing is nothing but, in this mechanical sequence of taking "the only step and the next step" (*Strangers*, p. 242), an effect of marking "Owen" and "Markman." ("Owen Markman" is just a bad play on words.)

This is the insistence of the letter in the unconscious—if, that is, communication media are the unconscious of the unconscious. The question then becomes, Why does the story of murder devolve so emphatically on the becoming-visible of writing as writing, on the transparency of media of communication? We have set out in some detail the media apriori of true crime. Here it is possible to extend the description of how vicarious life and vicarious crime indicate each other, via the mass media.

This is a matter, in part, of body transport and message transport, and their commutability.[31] On the plane en route to see Markman, Guy reads, among other things, a magazine clipping about himself—and experiences the familiar self-externalization and self-alienation of being-in-print. This self-alienation, however, is not merely self-distance. It is at the same time a registration of the way that the media enter into, and copy, self-reflection.

The Train, the Dictaphone, the Merry-Go-Round, and the Movies

Nietzsche, perhaps the first philosopher to write on the typewriter, wrote that "our writing instruments enter into our thoughts."[32] No doubt they enter into our thoughts about our writing instruments too—and this not least when writing loses its media monopoly over our thoughts and their transmission, and being-in-print (the identity program of print culture) yields to being-in-the-media.[33] Or, as Lacan more recently expressed these media links:

> From now on you are, and to far greater extent than you can imagine, subjects of gadgets or instruments—from microscopes to radio and television—which will become elements of your being. You cannot now understand the full significance of this; but it is nevertheless a part of the scientific discourse, insofar as discourse is something that determines a form of social cohesion.[34]

The yielding tie of subjects and gadgets, and the form of social cohesion it determines, center the closing scene of the novel. This is a scene of in-person confession in which, it turns out, both the personal and the confessional are handed over to their media doubles, gadgets and appliances. The scene, that is, binds together the shock experience of the machinery of the media and "the whole idea" for murder. It stages the shock modern life recoils from in its own realization. In doing so, it makes clearer how double minds, and double murder, realize the mass social bond.

Here is what the final scene looks like. Guy Haines has written out his confession, and, in the exchange with Markman, he is less speaking than playing back his words ("the words, unutterable thousands and thousands of words ... sentences and paragraphs of the confession")—or playing back the words of this guy's double[35]: "he had known the last words were coming ... it was exactly like Bruno" (*Strangers,* p. 249).

But the desire to confess in person at once comes up against Markman's "indifference." (Pressed on "[H]ow do you feel about the men you know who'd killed somebody," Markman beautifully responds, "Live and let live.") This indifference involves something more. Haines "groped for a concrete idea to present to Owen. He didn't want his audience to slip away" (*Strangers,* p. 251). And if a murder story would seem enough to hold "his audience"—not least in a detective novel about a murderer who "reads too many detective stories" and featuring a detective who sounds "like a radio detective" (p. 157)—what exactly does confessing to an audience mean?

The genre of confession instanced here is not hard to locate. The genre of deeply personal testimony presented to a mass audience has migrated from the novel to talk radio and confession TV. It posits a mass audience made up of listeners and viewers who "are included as excluded third parties, as 'parasites.'"[36] The media parasite is another name for vicarious life. Markmam here is a proxy for media third person: the one who—at once disengaged and watchful—observes what it looks like to react to situations and to observe and to communicate about oneself, one who listens, witnesses, and forgets.

Face-to-face confrontation is handed over to the media: "It was as if he talked to an inanimate thing like a dictaphone in the chair, the difference that his words didn't seem to be penetrating in any way" (*Strangers,* p. 250). The communication of a murder with "no personal motives"— about a double murderer broken down "with letters and blackmail" (p. 251)—is like speaking to a defective voice-recording, or voice-doubling, machine. But things are in fact more complicated still: his confession has been overheard by the detective who has followed him and tapped his telephone—although, as the detective explains, "There wasn't time for a dictaphone. But I heard most of it from just outside your door" (p. 255).

The apparatus, gratuitous but determinate, determines self-determination. The dictaphone, in the first instance, is a matter of analogy, a transfer of properties between persons and machine. The "human stupidity" of a "silent and motionless" (*Strangers,* p. 252) body (which cannot be penetrated and cannot set itself in motion and cannot register words) is set in contrast to the "intelligent silence of a live wire" (p. 255). To the extent that "life itself is but motion," the transfer of motion from persons to machines is the transfer of life itself.[37]

In the second instance, the technology is in place but strictly gratuitous: there but not hooked up. It is as if the reflexive machine returns as its own theme.[38] The media machine—as object and as instrument or relay—is simply there. (That hesitation stages what I have elsewhere called *the double-logic of prosthesis:* the machine as self-extension and self-extinction both.[39]) But the point not to be missed is that it is absolutely clear that the media apriori is already in place and operating anyway. The urge to confess has turned into something else: *the urge to confess has turned into the desire to be interviewed.*

The uncertain agency of media technologies here—the question of their effect and of their operation—is crucial. The difference between media analogy and media apriori is the difference between media copying, doubling, or "revealing" our situation, on the one side, and media "determining" our situation, on the other: the difference between analogy (we are like the machines we make) and cause (we are made by them).[40] This tension between likeness and determination is irreducible with respect to the experience of the psychotechnologies of everyday life.

There is no getting "back" of the communication of everyday life any more than there is a getting back of the reflexivity of the mass media— which means too that the social tie consists in its communication and nothing else.[41] It is not just that Guy sees his "mistake was in telling a stranger my private business" (*Strangers,* p. 246). Talking to strangers, in privatized public places like trains or hotel rooms, communicates the social tie—since the social tie consists in its communication and nothing else.

Guy had a horrible, an utterly horrible thought all at once, that he might ensnare Owen in the same trap that Bruno had used for him, that Owen in turn would capture another stranger who would capture another, and so on in infinite progression of the trapped and the hunted. (*Strangers,* p. 246)

This is the bare sociality of the chain letter. If, as we know, talking of love is itself a *jouissance,* if there is no "prediscursive" reality, if discourse is a form of social cohesion—then the social tie (like *McCall's* crusade for social "togetherness" in the name of "togetherness") consists of the "provocations that describe it as a social tie."[42] Communication or transmission resembles contagion: it transfers and communicates crime, effecting and deinvisibilizing a vicarious (parasitic and pathological) publicness.

That style of social bond is necessarily an unbinding tie, an asocial sociality. The paradox of sociality in the pathological public sphere means that the "acme of the 'sympathetic relationship' with others is simultaneously the ultimate nonrelationship with others: each imitates the 'every man for himself' of the others, here assimilation is strictly equivalent to a disassimilating dissimulation."[43] The public here is a disbanding band. Hence a second chain relation is communicated in this closing scene. This time the chain involves a transference not of guilt but of indifference—shared noncommunication and an estrangement of the publicness it effects: "What human being would inform on him. ... Everyone would leave it for someone else, who would leave it for someone else, and no one would do it" (*Strangers,* p. 253). The public, that is, consists of—to borrow the title of one of Highsmith's later novels—*those who walk away.*[44] This makes for the radically incoherent talk about "individual and society" that closes the novel, for example:

What business is it [murder, guilt] of mine? ... What business? Because you—you are part of society! Well, then it's society's business. ... Was that most people's attitude? If so, who was society? ... Society was people like Owen, people like himself ... people like you and me ... so far as people go. (*Strangers,* p. 252)

It makes for this incoherence in that it leaves the "and" of this duality "individual and society" uninterpreted and thus the unity of this complexity—which is the complex of vicarious crime and vicarious life—cannot be seen.

The social and self-reflexivity that we have been tracing—a new intensity of reflexivity, within and without—entails a "taking the role of the other" that borders on murderous violence: a Ripley-like identification and doubling to the point of "taking the place of the other." It entails an unremitting self-reflection bordering on self-violence. In that the individual in the modern sense is one who observes his or her own observation, identity yields to an uncontrollable identification.

In *Strangers on a Train,* and in Highsmith's writing generally, the reflexive idiom is the abnormally normal idiom of relation and self-relation: "The panic in the voice panicked Bruno" (*Strangers,* p. 74); "then in response to [his] friendly grin, he smiled too" (p. 76); "There was the sucking sound of a kiss … and Bruno gave it back to them" (p. 72). It extends to the nature of the world, the observed world: "As he looked, a bird flew out of the grass with a cry and wrote a fast, jagged, exuberant message with its sharp-pointed wings across the sky" (pp. 142–143). "Overhead a bird kept singing, 'Tweedledee?' and answering itself, 'Tweedle*dum!*'" (p. 153). Nature doubles culture and talks about doubles.

The popular technical media that mechanize images and double psychic life—media such as the train or the film—proliferate as the infrastructure of this world. The stranger—"the stranger on the train who would listen, commiserate, and forget" (*Strangers,* p. 23)—is one of the prototypes of modernity's stranger-intimacy and stranger-sociality—and of the media-referred belief that binds them.

Taking up these forms of intimacy, sociality, and belief means taking up the reality of things and images that move, and vanish, and repeat on schedule, like trains or movies.[45] It means taking up how people meet via the mass media of the motion industries, like trains and films, in a society tending toward a condition of total mobilization, and featuring mechanized motion, motives, and movies.

Consider, for example, the opening passage of *Strangers on a Train:*

The train tore along with an angry, irregular rhythm. It was having
to stop at smaller and more frequent stations, where it would wait
impatiently for a moment, then attack the prairie again. But the
progress was imperceptible. The prairie only undulated, like a vast,
pink-tan blanket being casually shaken. The faster the train went,
the more buoyant and taunting the undulations. (*Strangers,* p. 7)

Here again Highsmith's signature narration lends to fantasy the look of
objective description. The overexplicitness of the personation of technology
and topography makes for a psychotopography. This is at the same time a
framed scene viewed from the train window (a bit later too, and even more
explicitly, and in case we've missed it: "He could sense Miriam ahead of
him, not much farther now, pink and tan-freckled, and radiating a kind of
unhealthful heat, like the prairie out the window" [*Strangers,* p. 7]).

The tendency is to understand this scenario in terms of a reversal of
fantasy and reality. These are, for example, the terms drawn on in another
novel about machine transport and sexual violence, J. G. Ballard's *Crash:*
"In the past we have always assumed that the external world around us
has represented reality, and that the inner worlds of our minds, its dreams,
hopes, ambitions, represented the realm of fantasy and imagination. These
roles have been reversed."[46] But the psychotechnologies of everyday life,
like the train or the automobile, cannot simply, of course, be understood
as reversing fantasy and reality in that they enter into both. If our media
instruments enter into our thoughts, then our thoughts about them don't
exempt us from their effects. On the contrary: the becoming-visible of
these psychotechnologies is part of their functioning.

Strangers on a Train makes this as explicit as possible: "'Ever feel like
murdering somebody? ... I do. I'm sure sometimes I could kill my father.
... You know what my father does for a hobby? Guess. ... He collects
cookie cutters! ... The machine age!'" (*Strangers,* p. 17). The machine age,
to the extent that it makes itself from itself, to the extent that it mass-pro-
duces cookie-cutter individuals, dispenses with fathers, albeit violently.

Enduring autonomy like an alien command, the individual, like society, is freely and hopelessly delivered up to itself:

> "She's what people mean when they say America never grows up, America rewards the corrupt. She's the type who goes to the bad movies, acts in them, reads the love-story magazines, lives in a bungalow, and whips her husband into earning more money this year so they can buy on the instalment plan next year, breaks up her neighbour's marriage—"

> "Stop it, Guy! You talk so like a child!" (*Strangers,* p. 47)

It is not merely that the media are everywhere here (types, movies, cookie-cutter commuter suburbs, mass magazines, and so forth). The exposure of their penetration into every precinct of private and public life is itself spoken in the quoted idiom of the mass media ("they say," "I read somewhere people don't grow emotionally" [*Strangers,* p. 47]). And talking of the fact that America never grows up is to talk like a child: the exposure of the mechanism installs it.

The same goes for the injunction to "Stop it!" Or, as the panicked offscreen voice at the close of Hitchcock's film version of the novel puts it: "Get someone to stop this thing!" Vicarious life in *Strangers on a Train* is, we have seen, bound up through and through with technologies of communication and transmission. The psychotechnologies that mechanize images, double reality, and make up "double-track" minds appear, at bottom, as means of setting bodies, or persons, or machines in motion—as a matter of stopping or going.

The central questions here are about what sets persons in motion, what counts as motivation, and what is the reality of things that move. These no doubt timeless questions are made timely in relation to the modern motion industries of communication and transport.[47]

The motion industries are broadcast throughout the text. For example,

> Then he got up … that was coming just as it should. He felt he moved on certain definite tracks now, and that he could not have

stopped himself or got off them if he wanted to … he absolutely
had to do what he was going to do. … He wanted to keep moving.
He decided by the time he walked … it would be time to catch the
train. … He began to think of his course of action … he stopped.
… He hailed a cab. (*Strangers*, pp. 132–133)

The thing that needs to be stopped in Hitchcock's film version of
Strangers on a Train is a runaway merry-go-round. The merry-go-round—
one of the popular amusements of the machine age that couple still bodies
and moving machines[48]—is something like the central character in Hitchcock's movie. It is described in these terms in the novel:

The merry-go-round was like a lighted city in the dark woods, a
forest of nickel-plated poles crammed with zebras, horses, giraffes,
bulls, and camels all plunging down or upward, some with necks
arched out over the platform, frozen in leaps and gallops as if they
waited desperately for riders. Bruno stood still. (*Strangers*, p. 69)

The merry-go-round, that is, is nothing but a model of the technology of film itself—a light show in the dark, made up of stills of "frozen"
motion and suspended animation, about to be set in motion to music and
with the turning of the wheel, producing for stilled, immobilized, massed
viewers the uncertain and fugitive reality of moving pictures.

One anecdotal account of the origin of the coupling of physiological
and technical processes that makes that reality possible was the discovery
that telegraph or telephone poles observed from inside the window of a
moving train tended to "disappear" at the right speed, due to the psycho-
physiology of retinal fatigue and the afterimage,[49] hence the discovery of
the speed at which still frames might be moved to produce the mechanized
images of animation and motion. This amounts to the emitting to viewers
of their own processes of perception, such that act and observation fuse.[50]

One might perhaps take this a step further. To the extent that, by
this technical means, self-observation is installed as objective description,
Highsmith's narrative mode—which effects precisely that—might be said
to register just these psychotechnologies: to register the installation of the

cinema apriori of everyday life. If there is any doubt about this, consider the description of Guy Haines as he moves toward the scene of the murder he will commit, finding it "as if a curtain had lifted on a stage scene he already knew" and "as if he watched himself on a screen" (*Strangers*, p. 205). Written and prescripted and previewed plans are acted out, such that observation and act realize or play back each other. Haines moves at first, "stopping and going," and "mechanically," with the "feeling of moving on established tracks" (p. 135). He moves finally "on certain definite tracks": "Momentum," we are told, "smoothed his movements" (p. 133). In this astonishingly condensed description, the technical means by which momentum smooths movements, and thus animates them—the cinema—is at once effected and exposed. To the extent that that is the case, it becomes impossible to consider act and observation outside the situation of the media[51]: being-in-the-media is the mode and the model of vicarious life and vicarious crime.

The opening shot of Hitchcock's motion picture version of the novel films motion: moving feet, taxis, trains. In the scene in which Bruno and Guy talk about the no-motivation scheme of vicarious crime, the two sit at either end of the frame, which centers on the "view" outside the window of the moving train. But the view is of course a moving mirror, a film of that view playing on the screen/window before which the characters sit. "The technology of film," as one of its first theorists put it, "must dictate its own choice of content."[52] The stopping of the merry-go-round—in this film which is, from the opening shots on, a chase film, about stopping and going—is the stopping of the film mechanism itself.[53] The mechanized doubling of act and observation—the cinema apriori—is installed, as the double, or motive of the crime and as its modus operandi. Or, as Bruno puts it (in a coy doubling back of the novel on itself), "'I thought we'd do something nice. Maybe a good movie—with a murder in it—or maybe the amusement park" (*Strangers*, p. 99).

Notes

1. Patricia Highsmith, *The Talented Mr. Ripley* (1955; New York: Vintage, 1999), 150; subsequent references in the text abbreviated *Ripley*. On the

Highsmith/Ripley identification, see Andrew Wilson, *Beautiful Shadow: A Life of Patricia Highsmith* (London: Bloomsbury, 2004), 194–196.

2. Patricia Highsmith, *The Two Faces of January* (New York: Atlantic Monthly Press, 1964), 63.

3. On the function of the mass media as the background reality of modernity, see Niklas Luhmann, *The Reality of the Mass Media,* trans. Kathleen Cross (Stanford, CA: Stanford University Press, 2000); and Friedrich A. Kittler, *Literature, Media, Information Systems,* ed. John Johnston (Amsterdam: G + B Arts, 1997). I am in part in what follows tracing some of the implications of these rival accounts of the modern media apriori and testing out these rival idioms of analysis.

4. The contemporary form of this half-credence as to the constructed reality of the mass media means that, as Samuel Weber expresses it, "the paranoic element and the realistic element seem to work in tandem, reinforcing each other without providing any alternative sort of mediation." See Samuel Weber, in "Theory on TV: 'After-Thoughts,'" in *Religion and Media,* ed. Hent de Vries and Samuel Weber (Stanford, CA: Stanford University Press, 2001), 99. But if this "tandem" structure is irreducible, it may yet be possible to specify it beyond a generalized or overly rapid theorization of "mediation."

5. It is striking the extent to which deconstructive media theory has adopted this tabloid temporal urgency—"Today, more than ever before …" See Jacques Derrida, "Artifactualities," in Jacques Derrida and Bernard Stiegler, *Echographies of Television,* trans. Jennifer Bajorek (Oxford: Polity Press, 2002), 5. This urgency is coupled to its opposite: deconstructive media theory hesitates on attributing any deep difference at all to different materialities of communication (any new media appliance "reveals" a writing-in-general always already at work—albeit always now more than ever before). This coupling of urgency and timeless sameness indicates at the least a certain *stalling* in deconstructive media theory—or, as Friedrich Kittler more severely puts it, "technology is the blindspot of poststructuralism" (Kittler, *Literature, Media,* 8).

6. The notion of media "spin" that is, does not exhaust the panic/thrill that (as the ad for endless news puts it) "the world keeps spinning while you are sleeping, you know." On the systemic structure of media self-conditioning and self-exposure, see Luhmann, *Reality of the Mass Media,* 53–54, 33, et passim.

7. Patricia Highsmith, *Found in the Street* (New York: Atlantic Monthly Press, 1986), 6; hereafter in text abbreviated as *Found.*

8. Dirk Baecker, "The Reality of Motion Pictures," *MLN: Modern Language Notes* 111, no. 3 (1996): 561.

9. See chapter 3, "The Crime System." It is a world marked, that is, by second-order observing and secondhand nonexperience—just as a walk-on waitress in a recent J. G. Ballard novel, *Super-Cannes* (London: Flamingo, 2000), for example, wears a T-shirt with quotations from Baudrillard printed on it. And, after Kittler, one scarcely needs the 101st conference on the work of art in the age of mechanical doubling to report on that. But one might elaborate on the strange attraction of the media (as vicarious life) and crime (as vicarious performance and exchanged guilt) that structures that novel, among others. Ballard's most recent fiction are theses-novels about the relays between media and crime, and about those theses in turn as "paper-back sociology." J. G. Ballard, *Cocaine Nights* (London: Flamingo, 1996), 121. It is part of the form of knowledge, or knowingness, by which "media speculation is today's crucible of accepted truth." J. G. Ballard, *Millennium People* (London: Flamingo, 2003), 290.

10. Kittler, *Literature, Media*, 63.

11. Patricia Highsmith, *Plotting and Writing Suspense Fiction* (New York: St. Martin's Griffin, 1983), 88. Hence the person telling the story sits at a desk and types about Ripley, sitting at a desk writing and typing, making believe and making himself up. And, in real life, Highsmith, having written about this story of two persons—"one of whom kills the other and assumes his identity"—receives the Mystery Writers of America award for the novel. She recalls that on that award document "I lettered 'Mr. Ripley and' before my own name, since I think Ripley himself should have received the award. No book was easier for me to write, and I often had the feeling Ripley was writing it and I was merely typing" (*Plotting*, 75–76). (She would go on to "forge" Ripley's name on other documents as well.)

12. See my *Serial Killers: Death and Life in America's Wound Culture* (New York: Routledge, 1998).

13. Friedrich Schlegel, "Über Lessing," cited in Luhmann, *Art as a Social System*, trans. Eva M. Knodt (Stanford, CA: Stanford University Press, 2000), 287.

14. Patricia Highsmith, *A Suspension of Mercy* (1965; New York: Norton, 2001), 235, 155.

15. Patricia Highsmith, *The Cry of the Owl* (London: Heinemann, 1963), 7–8.

16. Patricia Highsmith, *Those Who Walk Away* (New York: Atlantic Monthly Press, 1967), 117.

17. Patricia Highsmith, *Strangers on a Train* (1950; New York: Penguin, 1979), 96; hereafter abbreviated as *Strangers*.

18. I am here drawing on Niklas Luhmann, "A Redescription of 'Romantic Art,'" *MLN: Modern Language Notes* 111, no. 3 (1996): 506–522—albeit pressuring, at the same time, the noncommunication between communicative systems (psychic and social) he posits. On that "uncanny" and gothicized intimation of communication, see also note 20, below.

19. In Highsmith, this is consistently the figure of a *dea ex machina* (the angelized woman)—Anne in *Strangers on a Train,* or the suicided wife in *Those Who Walk Away,* for example. On the gender-marking of the boundaries of modern technical, information, and media systems, see Friedrich A. Kittler, *Discourse Networks 1800/1900,* trans. Michael Meteer with Chris Cullens (Stanford, CA: Stanford University Press, 1990); and, with respect to the American scene, my *Bodies and Machines* (New York: Routledge, 1992) and *Serial Killers.*

20. Here we might say that the uncanny resemblance between psychic and social systems reenters the narrative—*as* the uncanny. Central is the manner in which the generalized experience of reflexivity devolves on horror and crime, and does so through an erosion of the boundaries between persons and media. Not least via the "rise of the machines" scenario, for example, that repeats in, or as, science fiction. The rise of the machines—the moment when, as one recent version enacts it: "What's the matter with the machines?" "I think they've become self-aware"—pressures the principle of scarcity with respect to reflexivity, and therefore with respect to personhood. (Or, as my son—age ten—put it, in watching a block of these science fiction episodes on television—"I *hate* it when they become self-aware!")

21. Friedrich Karl von Savigny, *System des heutigen romischen Rechts* (*System of Modern Roman Law*), vol. 2, trans. William Holloway (1840; Westport, CT: Hyperion Press, 1979), 206, 176.

22. Savigny, *System,* 179. For instance, the institution of the university, the corporation, or "the greatest and most important of all Juristical Persons: the Fiscus, that is to say the State itself" (p. 182).

23. Savigny, *System,* 210.

24. Savigny, *System,* 232. And it is worth recalling that the concept of personhood is itself "juristical" from the start: "Up until the early modern period, personhood remained an attribute mostly for legal relationships (but also relevant for existence as *civis* in a society, … Only in the eighteenth century was the concept of the individual tailored to persons, a refinement that transformed the concept of person at the same time." Niklas Luhmann, "The Mind and Communication," in *Theories of Distinction: Redescribing the Descriptions of Modernity,* ed. William Rasch (Stanford, CA: Stanford University Press, 2002), 183.

25. Savigny, *System,* 231.

26. Savigny, *System,* 231–233.

27. Savigny, *System,* 234–235.

28. On the coming into paradox of notions of the radical autonomy of the individual and the individual will, on the one side, and the self-contained society (which makes both individuals and their wills), on the other, see, for example, William Connolly, "The Will, Capital Punishment, and Cultural War," in *Cultural Studies and Political Theory,* ed. Jodi Dean (Ithaca, NY: Cornell University Press, 2000), 23–41. The paradox of "self and society," at this level, can simply be recycled, shifted from one side or the other, or "resolved" through metaphors such as mutual causality or transductive relation. I am suggesting that this paradox becomes intelligible and workable if we take up the reflexive condition of modern society and its media.

29. See chapter 3, "The Crime System." Cf. also Friedrich Kittler, "Romanticism-Psychoanalysis-Film: A History of the Double," in *Literature, Media,* 85–90; and Kittler, *Gramophone, Film, Typewriter,* trans. Geoffrey Winthrop-Young and Michael Wutz (Stanford, CA: Stanford University Press, 1999).

30. See Elena Esposito, "The Arts of Contingency," *Critical Inquiry* 31, no. 1 (Autumn 2004): 7–25.

31. I take up these "psychotechnologies of everyday life" in greater detail in chapter 6, "Berlin 2000: 'The Image of an Empty Place.'"

32. Friedrich Nietzsche, letter to Peter Gast (1882), cited by John Johnston in the introduction to Kittler, *Literature, Media,* 13.

33. There is a dense clustering of writing, recording, communicative media in these final pages. Such a drawing into relation of the becoming-visible of recording (the materialization of writing and the data stream, the writing of writing, and so on) and graphic violence is more or less canonical from the later nineteenth century on. On this radical entanglement of writing and violence—word counts and body counts—see my *Serial Killers.*

34. Jacques Lacan, *Le seminaire, livre XX: Encore?* (Paris: Editions du Seuil, 1975), 76.

35. The quickening of an experience of generality within could not be more explicit: "I meet a lot of guys—no pun—but not many like you" (*Strangers,* p. 27). At the same time, its *over*explicitness reduces to the self-disowning character of the cliché—by which the installation of the truth is bound up through and through with its self-exposure.

36. Luhmann, *Reality of the Mass Media,* 60. Luhmann is here drawing on Michel Serres's notion of the parasite, which he extends in these terms: "This consequently means that the mass media themselves are second-order

parasites, parasites which live parasitically on the parasiticality of their viewers"—that is, if one depathologizes parasitism and the addiction to the secondary. I set out a related but ultimately different account of the mass-media observer, by way of the genre of reality TV in chapter 7, "Postscript on the Violence–Media Complex (and Other Games)."

37. "Life it selfe is but motion" is Hobbes's formulation of the natural life of appetitive machines (persons). On motion and automatism in machine culture, see my *Bodies and Machines.*

38. These mechanically doubling machines are part of a self-reflexive media network—one that describes itself as a media network. The prototype of this apparently gratuitous but structurally determinate media machine is perhaps the daguerreotype apparatus in Hawthorne's *The House of the Seven Gables* (1852). There, in a scene of stopped narrative, a daguerreotype image is made of the dead body. But it is made with no clear purpose, in a moment of something like photography for photography's sake—yet it sets the narrative back in motion. Here too an apparently "extra" piece of technology, just *there,* seems to determine the situation. But why? What, more exactly, does this machine paradox indicate? For one thing, the image apparatus, as everyone by now knows, records death (the trace of what had been). Here, in doing so, it immediately generates something like a "modern" sphere of privacy and intimacy. This is an intimacy then bound from the start to a reflexive doubling via mechanical representation. This is something like the first "Kodak moment." Vicarious life through the media is bound to the mechanical operators of motion and stillness (in this novel, train, telegraph, daguerreotype). These mechanical doublers undo the identification of (natural) life with motion and generate (machinic) life. But there is more. The uncertain agency of the photograph in this scene is absolutely central to its functioning. It is not merely that the photographic act, in Hawthorne, immediately seems to evoke the by-now canonical relation between death and recording. The givenness of that relation conceals something else. This is the (temporal) uncertainty as to whether the photographic—the "it was"—exteriorizes a timeless relation between death and the media or marks a timely and media-specific one. The undecidability of this question does not settle the question. We can only communicate about and reflect on the media through media of communication and reflection. Hence the attempt to periodize media forms is itself bound to the question of the media. The question as to the periodization of the media returns periodically whenever "new media" enter the scene. But in that the media operate *via* rather than *despite* that paradoxicality, the media question is not exhausted in its being "put in question" (that is, its deconstruction).

The question concerning the media concerns how the media—that is, the media apriori, the media as system—enters into a *circuit of self-determination*. That is, what appears here—in the paradox of the gratuitously determinate dictaphone or camera—is the media paradox: *the self-generating* but also *self-exposing system* of the media. (See also note 40 below.)

39. See my *Bodies and Machines* (especially the final chapter, "The Love-Master").

40. Consider, for example, a movie such as Nicholas Roeg's *Don't Look Now.* Here it is impossible to tell whether the becoming-visible of the cinema apparatus (flashbacks, jump cuts, etc.) is a way of representing traumatic events, or the other way around, whether trauma is a way of registering (and personalizing) the cinema apriori. Nor does it help to identify camera and unconscious life, such that the cinematic in effect realizes what that life always already was (or, as the deconstructive media theorist Bernard Stiegler puts it: "plac[ing] myself ... under the authority of the critique proposed by Derrida ... we must posit the following hypothesis: life ... is always *already* cinema" (*Echographies,* 162). Stiegler borrows the term "transductive relation" to define this relation between image and life. But this is—to borrow Nietzsche's description of psychic pain—"really only a fat word standing in place of a skinny question mark." Deconstruction, it may be argued, refunctions all media as revelations, or exteriorizations, of writing-in-general. That's a good way to naivetize claims for the newness of new media. It also means that technology is of necessity the (self-theorized) blindspot of deconstruction. Even given the narrowness of academic citation circles, deconstructive media studies spin in a very tight orbit, playing back Derrida's "authorization" on an endless loop. More generally, it may be argued, the deconstruction of cinema undoes cinema. (If life is always already cinema, Plato's cavemen were already going to the movies.) There is no way, on these grounds, of deciding whether media "determine" our situation (Kittler) or "reveal" it (Derrida). Yet the uncertain agency of the media, in looking at films like *Don't Look Now,* seems to be exactly what is experienced at once as seductive and as traumatic.

41. The plot of *Strangers on a Train* is nothing but this doubling back on itself. The psychotechnologies of everyday life play back on an endless loop. This is named in crime fiction such as Jim Thompson's *Recoil* or Raymond Chandler's *Playback* or Cain's *The Postman Always Rings Twice* or *Double Indemnity.*

42. See Kittler, *Literature, Media,* 53.

43. See Mikkel Borch-Jacobsen, *The Emotional Tie: Psychoanalysis, Mimesis, and Affect,* trans. Douglas Brick (Stanford, CA: Stanford University Press, 1992), 33, 9.

44. In a short piece on what he calls "the negative power of collective behavior," Georg Simmel includes this note: "an English proverb says: 'The business of everybody is the business of nobody.' The peculiar fact that actions become negative once a plurality engages in them, is also shown in the motive in terms of which an attempt has been made at explaining the forbearance and indolence, in regard to public evils, of the (otherwise so energetic) North Americans. Public opinion there, the explanation runs, is supposed to bring about everything. Hence the fatalism which, 'making each individual feel his insignificance,' disposes him to leave to the multitude the task of setting right what is everyone else's business just as much as his own." Georg Simmel, "The Negative Character of Collective Behavior," in *The Sociology of Georg Simmel.* trans. and ed. Kurt W. Wolff (Glencoe, IL: Free Press, 1950), 396–401. Public opinion—or its double, popular psychology (the opinion or feeling of *no one* in particular)—is, for that very reason, the opinion or feeling of *everyone else,* which one can then cite and feel as one's own.

45. See Baecker, "The Reality of Motion Pictures." On the psychotechnology of film, from Munsterberg to Deleuze, see, among others, Kittler, *Gramophone, Film, Typewiter;* and Bernard Stiegler, *Technics and Time, 1: The Fault of Epimetheus,* trans. Richard Beardsworth and George Collins (Stanford, CA: Stanford University Press, 1998).

46. J. G. Ballard, introduction to the French edition, *Crash* (repr., New York: Vintage, 1974), 5.

47. And, along these lines, the panic of uncertain agency and the panic/thrill of the body–machine complex become indissociable.

48. On the merry-go-round in the machine age, see Bill Brown, *The Material Unconscious* (Cambridge, MA: Harvard University Press, 1996).

49. See Wolfgang Schivelbusch, *The Railway Journey: The Industrialization of Time and Space in the Nineteenth Century* (Berkeley: University of California Press, 1986).

50. On this "fusion" of act and observation—the technical form of second-order observation—see (in addition to Baecker and Kittler), Mark Hansen, *Embodying Technesis: Technology beyond Writing* (Ann Arbor: University of Michigan Press, 2000); Stiegler, *Technics and Time, 1,* and "The Discrete Image," in *Echographies of Television,* 147–163. One might consider too the range of psychoanalytic film theory by which psychic and filmic apparatus are taken to double each other (hence making film and its media specificity

simply redundant). Or one might consider, alternately, the visual history of "absorption and theatricality" that Michael Fried has compellingly traced. Here the techniques of the observer, and the techniques for observing non-observation, provide another way of understanding the media history of the forms of second-order observation—as art history.

51. Or, better, media rivalry, as I will take up in the next part of this book.

52. Paul Wegener, *Die Künstlerischen Möglichkeiten des Films* (1919), cited in Kittler, "Romanticism-Psychoanalysis-Film," 97.

53. The modern psychology of doubling—Otto Rank's Freudian account *The Double: A Psychoanalytic Study*—takes most of its examples (as Kittler traces) from films, without noticing it is going to the movies (just as the word "Kino"—movies, cinema—never appears in Freud's writing). At the same time, the film engineer Munsterberg puts in place the psychotechnology of film, which relies on a neurological precision that cannot be accessed "either by consciousness or language. Munsterberg assigns every single camera technique to an unconscious, psychical mechanism: the close-up to selective attention, the flashback to involuntary memory, the film trick to daydreaming, and so forth" (Kittler, "Romanticism-Psychoanalysis-Film," 100). There is an exact registration of this technical doubling of psychology and (transport/image) media in Hitchcock's description of his obsession with the "double chase motif": "In the ideal chase structure, the tempo and complexity of the chase will be an accurate reflection of the intensity of the relations between the characters. ... Griffith was the first to exploit the possibilities of a physical chase, but I tend to multiple chases and a lot of psychology." Cited in Donald Spolto, *The Dark Side of Genius: The Life of Alfred Hitchcock* (New York: Ballantine Books, 1983), 90.

CHAPTER 6

Berlin 2000

"The Image of an Empty Place"

Contemporary culture is full of reconstructions and reenactments—among these the return to the scene of the crime. The crime system and its fateful scenes: these hold steadily visible the reflexive intensities of modern social systems. There is, for one thing, the contingency of being under the unremitting observation of others—and of oneself. There is, along the same lines, the subjection of action and value to its self-reflection ("the reflexive monitoring of action"[1]). And there is too, then, the media doubling of the world (the media apriori) that sponsors both. True crime at once exposes and reflects on these forms of modern life and is thus part of their self-effecting operation. But the many returns, unhappy and not, to the scene of the crime have some further implications.

Figure 6.1

We know that a society that knows itself as "modern" organizes its ways of knowing along a timeline—the differences between past and future, early and late, not yet and no longer. It periodizes itself and does so via its technological media (from, say, print culture to the digital age).[2] Or, it parries the media apriori by deconstructing it.[3] Either way, a self-assessing modernity is bound to its media reflection, and that self-reflection is thus bound in turn to a sense of doubling back or afterwardness.

Here I want to take up this return to the scene of the crime—its reenactment and its reconstruction—by looking at a somewhat different zone of violence. My examples in this chapter are drawn from the volatile and phantasmic cityscapes that provide the social and cultural and psychic conditions of the linked experiences of modern violence and modern publicness.

The centering example is the "surrealestate" of the city of Berlin, its demolition, redemolition, and reconstruction. I consider then the more general woundscapes and scenes of the crime in which these experiences become legible. The intent is to test the forms of modern legibility and credibility that make up something like the reality show—the idioms of public belief and popular memory—of torn and reconstructed space.

In this chapter and the next, I turn, briefly, to the modeling of crime as play or game—and to the cold war games that provide exact models of that. In this part I take up the infrastructure of these cold war games, in three related ways. First, there is the destruction and remaking of the modern scene of the crime—a matter at once of memorializing and forgetting, reconstructing and erasing. Second, there is the manner in which this reenacted world is marked, above all, by the twinned forms of afterwardness in contemporary culture: the *traumatic* and the *forensic*. Third, there is the way in which publicness and violence are drawn into relation in the intricate scenes of a wound culture—public space and the site of violence, the scene of the crime, what might be described as a design flaw in the democratic invention.

Woundscapes

It has become a commonplace to say that the beauty of Berlin—if one can describe in that way a city whose essence is destruction—is its emptiness.

That emptiness is of course in large part a matter of wound and memory, violence and loss: the city's scarred identity as wound landscape and as the scene of the crime. But it is also, we know, much more than that.

For the architect Rem Koolhaas, for instance, this emptiness is a matter of the city's "efficiency": how "entirely missing urban presences or entirely erased architectural entities nevertheless generate what can be called an urban condition." For one thing, there are the hyper-visible efficiencies of the city: the everyday openness of the city of Berlin to its own infrastructure, its own nervous system. There is a basic difference between urban emptiness as loss that can be filled or replaced by architecture—even an architecture that monumentalizes loss or emptiness—and a postarchitectural city, one that cultivates its emptiness. The beauty of Berlin is, or was, at least in part, its *anti-architecture*: its vast quasioccupied areas of nothingness. On this view, the promise of Berlin, as "the most avant-garde European city," was the promise of the "postarchitectural city," an empty-center city.[4]

The promise was inseparable from destruction, and not least in that destruction itself was experienced as a precursor to, or even as a form of, urban planning. If Haussmann was Paris's "artist in demolition," total war was Berlin's. What urban planners represented and embraced as "the mechanical decongestant of bombing and the final battle"—the annihilation, or de-densification, of the center of the city—was something like the technical production of Berlin's "newest rubble architecture."[5] For this reason, it was possible to maintain that "total war must be seen not only as the end of the Third Reich, but also as the precursor to reconstruction."[6] Or, as Friedrich Kittler has argued (by way of Thomas Pynchon's total war novel, *Gravity's Rainbow*), the carpet bombings of the city belonged to some secret history of urban design: "each shockwave plotted in advance to bring *precisely tonight's wreck* into being ... it is in working order."[7]

The reconstruction of the last decade or so reworks these relays of devastation and preservation. The reconstructed city tends toward, on one side, an erasure of the past in the world-corporate architecture of the posthistorical city unimpressed by time. It tends, on the other, to a mechanical self-preservation: "the result of a gigantic attempt to make it the museum of its own past, a museum not of originals but of *Blade-Runner*-like replicated reality." In the narrow interim between reconstruction and reoccupation as the new capital, the empty-centered city has appeared at times as a "brand-new ghost town": for an interval, a Brasilia at the heart of the new Europe.[8]

That emptiness, in short, is now being reoccupied at an astonishing pace. The large areas of openness that have defined the cratered and divided postwar city are disappearing, as Berlin is being torn and reconstructed to take over as the synthetic capital and ersatz representation of the newly reunified Germany in the year 2000.

A look at the situation of Berlin, its empty places and lethal spaces, can begin to indicate then some of the relays between scene and crime, space and wound, place and identity, that will occupy me here. For what has the open or empty space of the city—the romance of an anti-architecture— come to mean? And what exactly does it mean for these empty spaces, for empty space, to disappear? "The architecture of redevelopment," the critic Rosalyn Deutsche observes, "constructs the built environment as a medium, one we literally inhabit, that monopolizes popular memory by controlling the representation of its own history. It is truly an evicting architecture."[9] But what, more precisely, is being evicted here? And what replaces it?

The Love Parade

One of the annual events that take place in Berlin each July, in the years since the reunification, is a mass gathering called the Love Parade (an event that has now spread to several other European capitals). Nominally a political event—the city picks up the trash—hundreds of thousands of people move to, gather at, and fill the vacant center of the city to the rhythmic, sampled machine beat of techno. The vast massing of the population without a direct object—unlike the nationalist Bastille Day and retro-nationalist World Cup massings that took place in Paris around the same time as the 1998 parade—seems in Berlin a demonstration of something strange and, perhaps, something new: a demonstration of the very possibility of a mass gathering without a direct national or political referent.

Figure 6.2

That is to say, a resolutely peaceful and festive massing of the public that *seems to hold the place of the very possibility of "the public" itself.*

Things are, of course, more complex. In the few years since the first small populist Love Parade, corporate sponsorship of the event has moved in. And the slogan of 1998's parade, for instance—"One World, One Future"—might be read as the new corporate logo of the world-corporation city under construction: the new federal architecture rivaled and mirrored by corporate monuments such as the Sony Center and Daimler building near the razed and reoccupied Potsdamer Platz.

The slogan of unity itself has of course, too, powerful resonances in this place: the writer François Mauriac memorably remarked that he loved

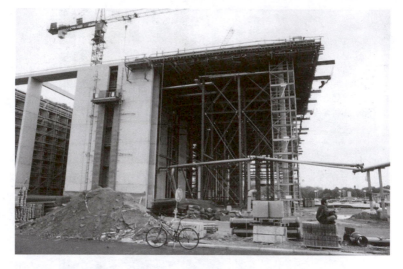

Figure 6.3

Germany so much he was glad there were two of them. For a half century there has been an unrelaxed insistence on rewriting "Deutschland über alles" as (in Hans Magnus Enzensberger's alternative slogan) "Germany, Germany—among other things."

But if the Love Parade gathering had perhaps acquired some of the markers of corporate publicity or (in Stuart Hall's phrase) "authoritarian populism," it may, beyond that, tell us a bit more about the status of public spaces, their opening, and their appropriation.[10]

The "One World, One Future" captioning of the Love Parade might be taken, alternatively, as an emblem of what the political philosopher Claude Lefort calls "the loving grip of the good society." For Lefort, this is the *negative* formula for the retreat of the political and the *lapsing* of a democratic politics. This is because, for Lefort, "the important point is that democracy is instituted and sustained by the *dissolution of the markers of certainty*. It inaugurates a history in which people experience a fundamental indeterminacy as to the basis of power, law, and knowledge, and as to the basis of relations between *self* and *other*."[11] The radical mutation inaugurated in the form of society that Tocqueville called "the democratic invention" was the elaboration of a social order that structures itself by itself. On this logic, there is nothing deeper than the "groundless ground" of a strictly indwelling network of relations of power and knowledge. This is a society "without a body … a society which undermines the representation of an organic totality": as the by-now default and quasiautomatic refrain goes, "radically open, contingent, incomplete."[12] Without basis or foundation, "groundless ground," disembodied, undermined: this is the idiom of an anti-architecture. Its image is not that of the loving grip of the good society. It is instead what Lefort calls "the image of an empty place."[13]

The ghostly or phantom-like character of the public and the public sphere is, on this view, precisely the point. It is not something to be exorcised or congealed into a fixed place or coerced into an organic identity: it is the phantom condition of the public as such.[14]

There are two risks here, both of which are mapped in high relief on the Berlin landscape. The first ("One World, One Future," for instance) is that of an unequivocal identification, which gives rise to an identity politics. The second risk—in effect, an endorsement of equivocation, an abiding in ambivalence, openness, contingency, and incompletion tout court—is that no name whatsoever can be given either to the political or to the subject.[15] If the first threatens to make Berlin into a sort of Architecture-of-Democracy Mall, the second promises to make of it something like a Theme Park of the Uncanny. This deadlock—the compulsive pas de deux between a corporatism in the name of democracy and a self-evacuating style of postmodernism—has become familiar enough. It is nowhere more visible than in the projects for reconstructing Berlin.

Democratic Social Space

Consider the debate about a "representative" architecture for the city. This is not merely a debate about what this architecture should represent, what an editor of *Der Spiegel* called "the dream of representative buildings."[16] It is a debate about whether places, including empty ones, mean or represent anything at all, about, in the architect Bernard Tschumi's words, "the idea of a meaning immanent in architectural structures."[17] The dream of representative buildings is countered by a dream of emptying structures of significance.

The relentlessly self-effacing architecture of the interim capital, Bonn, resisted not merely a particular symbolic style but the imposition of any symbolism as such. Hence it is argued, in the reconstruction debates, that "architecture in a democracy need not be faceless"; that "symbolism in architecture need not be synonymous with the Third Reich."[18] What becomes visible here is what Deleuze and Guattari have called "the face-system" and its "face-landscape correlations": "Architecture positions its ensembles—houses, towns, or cities, monuments or factories, to function like faces in the landscape they transform."[19] The face-system that correlates place and identity—that produces what might be called place-identity—gothicizes space and personates place.

It is not difficult to see how these debates restage two related fallacies or fantasies. I am referring, first, to the genetic fallacy: the notion that where things come from can tell us what they are or what they mean—which is the fallacy at the bottom of identity politics and its complement, trauma studies. I am referring, second, to its counterside, the republican fantasy: the desire to come from nowhere, to give birth to oneself. I have traced these tendencies at some length elsewhere.[20] For now, we may note that, at its most reductive, one rediscovers in these debates a resistance to meaning-as-such as a resistance to power-as-such—a kind of pop-Foucauldianism that also has become familiar enough.

Here is a brief sampling of how place-identity functions across these sites. The dream of representative buildings has meant, most visibly, the drawing on expanses of transparent glass to express openness and accessibility: the glass wall as an emblem of democratic transparency. This is in part carried over from the insistently understated and self-effacing federal architecture of the interim capital, Bonn, an architecture that, erasing the fascist period, referred backward to a prefascist and exiled Bauhaus style, even as a "Bauhaus-inspired modernism had become the house style for corporate America in the late 1950s and 1960s."[21] It functions as a response, too, to the emphatically paradoxical situation of the free city for decades entirely encircled by, and defined by, an imprisoning dead wall. The appeal is to a direct equivalence between transparent facades and democratic public space, an exorcism of the ghosts of fascism through the construction, for example, of a new type of dome on the Reichstag—a glass lighthouse for democracy redesigned by the British (that is, not German) architect Sir Norman Foster.

One difficulty is that such crystal palaces have for more than a century served as the architecture of commercialism and have come to represent, more recently, a self-referential, self-reflective corporatism. Another difficulty is the counterassociation of a politics of transparency; for instance, the Casa del Fascio (House of Fascism) built for Mussolini by Giuseppi Terragni: "A glass house in which everyone can peer, giving rise to the architecture that is the complement of this idea: no encumbrance, no barrier, no obstacle between the political hierarchy and the people."[22] In Manfredo Tafuri's terms, "Glass—the synthesis of matter and the immaterial, the symbol of the transparency of the subject with respect to collectivity"—that is, the spatial projection of a sheer identification of the people and the state.[23]

There are further difficulties, of a different order. The Berlin architecture of democracy-made-visible has a hyperexplicitness about it, suspending the belief that it posits. As one urban designer puts it, "[W]e want to create the impression that we have nothing to hide"; as another expresses it, the intent is to create "only a feeling of openness."[24] For the glass-wall federal building in Bonn, too small to accommodate a gallery, bleachers were erected so that citizens could view their representatives at work in their name through the glass. For the new capital buildings, bulletproof glass is incorporated into the designs. The glass dome set on top of the reconstructed Reichstag is filled with a pair of spiral viewing ramps, open to visitors when the Bundestag is in session.

This is a see-through democracy, in several senses: democracy made visible and public space as spectacle: in effect, as safe zone from the public it at once represents, images, and evicts. The public/private divide, in all its normalcy and in all its incoherence, is what is at issue, what trembles, in these proliferating designs. There is, for one thing, the relentless proliferation of pseudopublic, or privatized public, spaces: the overlit atrium of the gathering population epitomized by the privatized public space of the mall.[25]

Writing on that peculiar institution, the hotel lobby, Siegfried Kracauer observes that the determining togetherness of this social space means that the guests are "guests in space tout court—a space that encompasses them and has no function other than to encompass them." It posits a stranger-intimacy that "signifies only its own emptiness": the "inessential foundation" of an abstract and formal equality. On this modeling of democracy as the image of an empty place, the individual is "reduced to a 'member of society as such' who stands superfluously off to the side."[26]

This space seems a rehearsal for the symbolic architecture I have been imaging. The Reichstag's interior was gutted but the exterior preserved in a way that, as its architect Foster expressed it, left the structure "present but void." At the center of the Sony Center, still under construction when I first saw it (March 2000), there is, suspended in the impressive atrium, an enormous empty sphere: in effect, the monumentalization of an encompassing but voided space. This is a paramnesic symptom of the democratic idea: placeholder and disavowal at once.

There is one final "turn" in the proliferation of such images of an empty place in Berlin. Throughout the wounded city, one rediscovers projects that attempt a localization of memory in memorialization, the erasure of history in its monumentalization. These are attempts, as Michael Wise has written, to "heal the wounds" of the city as a way to heal its inhabitants of "the malady of being German": ways of constructing a "final solution to Germany's memorial problem."[27] One project, initially rejected as a central memorial to the victims of the Reich, was the scheme designed by Richard Serra and Peter Eisenman. It consisted of 4000 wall-like concrete slabs, arranged like a vast burial ground.

If the erasure of what had been erased consists of an erasure of the past in the name of history, this project was seen as the permanent creation of what former chancellor Kohl called an "open wound in central Berlin": a wound, in effect, as its own monument.

The Mimesis of Publicness

The common places of a wound culture could not be more visible and more explicit than here, in the excruciated and self-excavating debates about Berlin's reconstruction. In the contemporary pathological public sphere, pain, trauma, damage, and the wound have become the self-authorizing indices of the real, both historical and psychic. But it is not difficult to detect how these collective probings of the wound are, by now, a little *too* self-evident, as if deferring belief in what is at the same time affirmed, as if serving as a sort of placeholder for something else.

That something else is the contemporary form of the public sphere, in which publicness and pathology have become indissociable. It is not merely that the mourning thing—the trauma apriori—has emerged as something like an infomercial of the psychic order or, at the least, of the modern soul. The wound and its strange attractions have come to function as a relay point of psychic and social orders, a way of locating and cathecting social space. This is a public sphere bound to shock, trauma, and damage, an opening or gaping toward others as the principle of (psychical) relation to an other and (social) relation to others.

The notion that in modernity public and private communicate in the wound may by now be a commonplace. But that communication remains to be specified. For Walter Benjamin, for example, following Simmel and Freud, the modernist experience is an experience at once of mechanical reproducibility and of shock or trauma[28]; trauma, by extension, is something like mechanical reproducibility housed in persons. Along these lines, the recent turn to the trauma apriori serves as a proxy for the absence of

Figure 6.4

a compelling idiom by which public and private, the historical and the psychical, might find their point of contact in contemporary culture.

I have taken up this line of inquiry elsewhere[29]; here, my concerns are somewhat different. The decline of the "aura" in machine culture, for Benjamin, is, more exactly, its "ultimate retrenchment" in the "fleeting expression of the human face." The face is the "focal point" of early photography. For Benjamin, this gives way, around 1900, to another photographic image: the exhibition of eerily empty or deserted city streets. Instancing Atget's photographs, Benjamin observes, we recall, that "it has justly been said of him that he photographed them like scenes of the crime. The scene of the crime, too, is deserted; it is photographed for the purpose of establishing evidence."[30] No doubt there is a policial aspect to these images. But what surfaces here is perhaps something more: something like a resemblance between the face and scene of the crime. "No face is surrealistic to the same degree," Benjamin elsewhere notes, "than the true face of a city."[31] The disturbance in the relations between personality and space—the condition of the torn and open subject of the pathological public sphere—is nowhere clearer than in the image of an empty place as the scene of crime and of a wounded sociality both.

Hence what I have been tracing, by way of the situation of Berlin, are in effect two versions of the urban afterimage that are also, and crucially, two versions of the condition of publicness today: the traumatic and the forensic. I want to close by unpacking a bit these versions of the sociality of the wound and by making clearer how notions of urban credibility— that is, the credibility of collective life—are relayed by torn scenes such as the city of Berlin.

The trauma apriori should by now be clear enough. One might say that the repressive hypothesis (by which the entire culture, according to Foucault, turned to the confession of sex) has been given over to the trauma hypothesis (by which the entire culture has turned to the confession of wounds and victimage). What has been described as the emergence of a "new victim" order, an order that proceeds under the sign of an ecumenical pathos, amounts to the positing of the sociality of the wound: *collectivity in commiseration*.[32] Hence, the by-now compulsively repeated commonplaces about, for example, "the ghosts of Berlin," its "haunted" character, and the debates as to the manner in which a "building or monument might be able to display the wounds of Berlin's past."[33]

The forensic apriori proceeds along somewhat different lines. The forensic appeals as well to the afterwardness of violation and to the "aftermath" character and "always already" foreclosure of scene and event. (It is as if the deconstructive logo—*déjà toujours*—was something of a placeholder for both the traumatic and the forensic turn) Beyond that, the forensic way of seeing pathologizes, or criminalizes, public space. If the term "forensic" is itself derived from "forum," with its sense of public meeting and collective exchange, forensic realism couples publicness and crime in a generalized fantasy of surveillance. It posits the everyday openness of every body to detection and places every area of urban life under suspicion. It operates, that is to say, in the film noir idiom of an "ecology of fear": the urban scene as crime scene.

Consider, for example, the 1997 Los Angeles exhibition of California art called "The Scene of the Crime." Instancing what Ralph Rugoff, the curator of the exhibition, calls an "aesthetic of aftermath," this forensic art updates Atget's deserted city streets as the scene of the crime with its multiplication of deteriorated, defaced, and abandoned architecture; depopulated and evacuated interiors; emptied places and torn spaces. This is the imaging of the forensic—public scene and crime scene—in the image of an empty place.[34]

It is not difficult to detect what such afterimages look like and what, in turn, they make visible. For one thing, one may detect here a becoming-visible of something like the radical ("new") historicist conviction that there is nothing more to the interiority of the subject than its formation from the outside in—the subject produced and evacuated at once, such that the socialization of the subject, and its traumatization, are two ways of saying the same thing. The at once solid and emptied spatial interiors that define, for example, the extraordinary work of the British sculptor Rachel Whiteread—the solidification of vacated interiors, the congealing of negative space—provides an exact counterpart of these psychotechnic modelings of place and identity, psychic and collective.

But it is just this congealing of democracy-as-empty-place into an image that returns us to the problem of the newly renovated "synthetic" metropolis as replica or theme park or reality show: to social symbolic space as, in effect, a ready-made. The synthetic metropolis distributes across its landscapes ready-made versions of intimacy and publicness, putting in place, here and there, interactive replicas of its own condition, a perpetual reality show. The ready-made has been seen to "ratify the self-sufficiency of reality and the definitive repudiation, by reality itself, of all representation."[35] But it may, of course, be seen to ratify just the reverse: the definitive repudiation, in the self-sufficiency of representation itself, of all reality. For if the reality show, from one point of view, represents nothing but a drive to restock the depleted hunting grounds of the real with artificial game, it represents, from another, "the true ambition of the Metropolis": "to create a world totally fabricated by man, i.e., to live *inside* fantasy."[36]

The synthetic metropolis responds to the fear of not getting enough reality with ersatz models of authenticity—not least, in rehearsals of violence and violation as markers of "the real." It responds to the fear of not getting enough pleasure with models of surrogate or referred intimacy. In short, it responds to the incredulity with respect to the reality of any social bond or collective life with the public reality show and its interactive compulsions.

In the mimesis of publicness, the citizens of the synthetic metropolis are guests in space tout court: a space in which the entire population can play the part of extras. It is difficult not to see the glass-house architecture of the Reichstag dome in terms of such a mimesis of publicness. But the point not to be missed is the way in which such public spaces at the same time resonantly and evocatively function as placeholders of the democratic invention.

The contemporary pathological public sphere posits precisely *the sociality of the wound*: the *public and collective gathering* around trauma, crime, and damage. Along these lines, Los Angeles's "Scene of the Crime" exhibition might be seen in relation to other urban-shock shows such as the Saatchi "Sensation" show or the 1998 exhibition of Stockholm's Moderna Museet called "Wounds: Between Democracy and Redemption in Contemporary Art."[37] Here, too, torn and opened bodies and torn and open spaces relay—on the model of referred pain—the referred intimacies and referred beliefs that are the condition of urban collectivity and urban credibility today.[38]

There is a good deal more to be said about such *Stimmungsarchitektur* (mood architecture) of democracy and about such social and cultural scenes in which an unremitting scarring and a perpetual state of emergency are experienced as communality.[39]

But let me end for the moment with one last small example. In fall 2000, the exhibition assembled by the Moderna Museet of post-1989 artwork by artists of the formerly communist Eastern Europe, "After the Wall: Art and Culture in Post-Communist Europe," will have had as its final destination the Hamburger Bahnhof in Berlin. What centers the exhibition are depleted and voided and absent sites: images of empty and emptied places. What these afterimages now will have come to look like, in a city unremittingly referred back to itself and its wounded premises, yet remains to be seen.

Figure 6.5

Notes

1. See Anthony Giddens, *The Consequences of Modernity* (Stanford, CA: Stanford University Press, 1990).
2. One sign of that is the shift in the terms of periodization thinking from "society" to "culture."
3. That is, the deconstruction of media difference through its generalization: the succession of media forms appear then as the difference-engine of the world—"writing-in-general."
4. Rem Koolhaas, interviewed by Hans Ulrich Obrist, "On the Current Urban Reconstruction in Berlin," *Feed* (1998), http://www.feedmag.com/re/re114.2.html.
5. See Wolfgang Schivelbusch, *In a Cold Crater: Cultural and Intellectual Life in Berlin, 1945–1948,* trans. Kelly Barry (Berkeley: University of California Press, 1998), 14–15; and Friedrich Kittler, "Unconditional Surrender," in *Materialities of Communication,* ed. Hans Ulrich Gumbrecht and K. Ludwig Pfeiffer (Stanford, CA: Stanford University Press, 1994), 324. The surrealestate of the postwar city made visible everywhere "the ruins of uncanny life": "a room cut in half sways at a height above the abyss of a courtyard filled with rubble; hopelessly isolated in the wasteland of rubble of an executed quarter, with a table, piano, sofa, chairs, and both walls hung with pictures ... from behind the curtains of this deserted world, a woman emerges from an invisible backdoor on to the stage, groping along the table ... borne aloft for a moment." Johannes R. Becher, "Deutsches Bekenntnis," quoted in Schivelbusch, *In a Cold Crater,* 19. In this state of suspension, there is "something artificial about such preservation amid the general devastation, like something put together for an exhibition." Johannes R. Becher, "Deutsches Bekenntnis," quoted in Schivelbusch, *In a Cold Crater,* 21.
6. W. Durth, *Deutsche Architekten: Biographische Verflechtungen 1900–1970* (Braunschweig, 1986), 15.
7. Kittler, "Unconditional Surrender," 325. Thomas Pynchon, *Gravity's Rainbow* (New York: Viking Press, 1973), 520–521. See also Mike Davis, "Berlin's Skeleton in Utah's Closet," *Grand Street* 69 (Berlin issue): 92–105; and "Theory and Praxis: Berlin," including essays by Alan Colquhoun, Manfredo Tafuri, and Joan Ockman, in *Architecture, Criticism, Ideology,* ed. Joan Ockman (Princeton, NJ: Princeton Architectural Press, 1985).
8. See Schivelbusch, *In a Cold Crater,* 186.

9. Rosalyn Deutsche, "Architecture of the Evicted," *Strategies* 3 (1990): 176. See also Rosalyn Deutsche, *Evictions: Art and Spatial Politics* (Cambridge, MA: MIT Press, 1996).

10. Stuart Hall, "Popular-Democratic vs Authoritarian Populism: Two Ways of Taking Democracy Seriously," in *The Hard Road to Renewal: Thatcherism and the Crisis of the Left* (London: Verso, 1988), 123–149.

11. Claude Lefort, "The Question of Democracy," in *Democracy and Political Theory* (Minneapolis: University of Minnesota Press, 1988), 19.

12. See Lefort, "The Question of Democracy," 18; and Deutsche, *Evictions*, 303.

13. Claude Lefort, "The Logic of Totalitarianism," in *The Political Forms of Modern Society: Bureaucracy, Democracy, Totalitarianism* (Cambridge, MA: MIT Press, 1986), 279.

14. See *The Phantom Public Sphere,* ed. Bruce Robbins (Minneapolis: University of Minnesota Press, 1993). On some of the risks involved in endorsing the spectral and radically open *tout court* (that is, in endorsing a politics of the designifier), see note 15, below.

15. The opening of bodies and persons to public experience is perhaps intimated in the very notion of the public sphere as *Öffentlichkeit,* openness (the etymological root of Habermas's word for the public sphere). But I have in mind here something other than the overly hasty theorization of "openness" that has governed some recent work on the culture and politics of the urban scene: for instance, Edward Soja's formulaic reiteration of a democratizing "radical openness" or Rosalyn Deutsche's compelling, Lefortian theorization of a logic of eviction, which yet similarly lapses in the direction of a general and "radical openness." See Edward W. Soja, *Thirdspace: Journeys to Los Angeles and Other Real-and-Imagined Places* (Oxford: Blackwell, 1996); Deutsche, *Evictions*, 324–327. It may be that the democratic invention posits a politics without foundation. But if the democratic invention is without foundation—if it is of necessity uncertainly premised on the openness of an empty place—an abstracted anti-foundationalism does not equal democracy. The (pop)deconstructive turn here, from the object to its theorization, risks the petrification of the idea of democracy—its congealed idealization—in the name of just the opposite, a radical openness. That is, the defetishizing groundlessness of the democratic invention is thus itself fetishized, congealed and idealized by way of a simple logic of equivalence between openness and democracy. (Hence it becomes necessary, for example, for Michael Sorkin, in the introduction to a recent collection of essays on the "politics of propinquity," to issue a reminder that "it is most likely because public space is so often and so

readily conceived as dependent on a decorporealization of its citizenry—a demotion and even denigration of the particular and the physical—that the notion of public space has become so *abstract*, so divorced from any theorization of physical locations." Michael Sorkin, "Introduction: Traffic Democracy," in *Giving Ground: The Politics of Propinquity*, ed. Joan Copjec and Michael Sorkin (New York: Verso, 1999). The irreducibility of the public sphere to physical place does not mean that place simply gives ground to a rhetoric of groundlessness. This is, in effect, to evict the democratic invention by way of endorsing democracy as eviction tout court.

16. Mathias Schreiber, "Selbstdarstellung der Bundesrepublik Deutschland," in *Staatsrepräsentation*, ed. Jörg-Dieter Gauger and Justin Stagl (Berlin: Dietrich Reimer Verlag, 1992), 203.

17. Tschumi, quoted in Denis Hollier, *Against Architecture: The Writings of Georges Bataille*, trans. Betsy Wing (Cambridge, MA: MIT Press, 1989), xi.

18. Quoted in Michael Z. Wise, *Capital Dilemma: Germany's Search for a New Architecture of Democracy* (Princeton, NJ: Princeton Architectural Press, 1998), 37, 61. I am here and elsewhere, indebted to Wise's account.

19. Gilles Deleuze and Félix Guattari, *A Thousand Plateaus*, trans. Brian Massumi (Minneapolis: University of Minnesota Press, 1987), 172.

20. See my *Serial Killers: Death and Life in America's Wound Culture*, esp. chapter 4.

21. Wise, *Capital Dilemma*, 29.

22. Quoted in Thomas Schumacher, "Giuseppe Terragni: Political and Other Allegories," in *The Architecture of Politics: 1910–1940*, ed. Samuel C. Kendall (Miami Beach, FL: Wolfsonian Foundation, 1995), 48.

23. Manfredo Tafuri, "U.S.S.R.–Berlin 1922: From Populism to 'Constructivist International,'" in Ockman, *Architecture, Criticism, Ideology*, 131.

24. Walter Karschies, quoted in Wise, *Capital Dilemma*, 85.

25. See Mike Davis, "Urban Renaissance and the Spirit of Postmodernism," in *Postmodernism and Its Discontents: Theories, Practices*, ed. E. Ann Kaplan (London: Verso, 1988), 87; Meaghan Morris, "Great Moments in Social Climbing: King Kong and the Human Fly," in *Sexuality and Space*, ed. Beatriz Colomina (New York: Princeton Architectural Press, 1992), 1–52; and Deutsche, *Evictions*, esp. "Agoraphobia," 269–327.

26. Siegfried Kracauer, "The Hotel Lobby," in *The Mass Ornament: Weimar Essays*, trans. Thomas Y. Levin (Cambridge, MA: Harvard University Press, 1995), 173–185.

27. Wise, *Capital Dilemma*, 154.

28. Walter Benjamin, "The Work of Art in the Age of Mechanical Reproduction," in *Illuminations,* ed. Hannah Arendt and trans. Harry Zohn (New York: Harcourt, Brace, and World, 1969), 226; "Surrealism," in *Reflections,* ed. Peter Demetz and trans. Edmund Jephcott (New York: Harcourt, Brace, and Jovanovich, 1978), 182.

29. See my *Serial Killers: Death and Life in America's Wound Culture,* esp. part 4, "Wound Culture: Trauma in the Pathological Public Sphere."

30. Benjamin, "The Work of Art," 226.

31. Benjamin, "Surrealism," 182.

32. I am drawing here on Jean Baudrillard, *The Perfect Crime,* trans. Chris Turner (London: Verso, 1996), 131–141.

33. See Brian Ladd, *The Ghosts of Berlin: Confronting German History in the Urban Landscape* (Chicago: University of Chicago Press, 1997), 235.

34. See Ralph Rugoff, Introduction and "More than Meets the Eye," in *Scene of the Crime* (Cambridge, MA: MIT Press, 1997), 12–22, 59–108.

35. Manfredo Tafuri, "Toward a Critique of Architectural Ideology," repr. in *Architecture Theory since 1968,* ed. K. Michael Hays (Cambridge, MA: MIT Press, 1998), 18.

36. The first position is epitomized by the work of Baudrillard, the second by the work of Koolhaas. (See, for example, Rem Koolhaas, "'Life in the Metropolis' or 'The Culture of Congestion,'" repr. in *Architecture Theory since 1968,* 323–330.) There is no richer representation of the radical entanglement of these positions and their architectural idiom than the fiction of J. G. Ballard, from the 1970s novel *High-Rise* to the recent *Cocaine Nights.* As Ballard puts it, in tracing these alternating currents of the real: "a new social type was being created by the apartment building, a cool, unemotional personality impervious to the psychological pressures of high-rise life, with minimal needs for privacy, who thrived like an advanced species of machine in the neutral atmosphere. ... Alternatively, their real needs might emerge later. ... In many ways, the high-rise was a model of all that technology had done to make possible the expression of a truly 'free' psychopathology." J. G. Ballard, *High-Rise* (New York: Holt, Rinehart, and Winston, 1975).

37. See the exhibition catalogue essays, *Wounds: Between Democracy and Redemption in Contemporary Art* (Exhibition Catalogue No. 268, Moderna Museet Stockholm, 1998). For the exhibition curator, David Elliott, the singularity or "autonomy" of the wound represents the "individual path" that counters modern "collectivism": "Wounds, it could be argued, result from the incompatibility of democracy with individual freedom or redemption" (Elliott, "No Pain No Gain," *Wounds,* 10–16). This is exactly

to mistake what I have been describing as the sociality of the wound in contemporary culture—the *convening* of the public around sites of damage and violation. Or, in Bataille's terms, "Human beings are never united with each other except through tears and wounds" (Quoted in Denis Hollier, *Against Architecture*, 67–68). Something like this case is made in Nancy Spector's contribution to the catalogue ("Subtle Bodies," *Wounds*, 89–93), which explicitly draws on the notion of a "wound culture" I have been elaborating.

38. The condition of referred intimacy and referred belief might be seen to structure as well a good deal of the style of commentary that relays these culture scenes. Hence Rugoff, in "More Than Meets the Eye" (*Scene of the Crime*), repeats the notion that in the face of such art "one's reassuring belief in a moral and rationally ordered universe was rudely imperiled" (p. 68); that it produces a "violent disruption of conventional 'reality'"; that this art image is "no longer a mere container … no longer simply looked at … no longer an ideal viewing position" (pp. 72–73). Hence Arthur Danto, in a review of the "Sensation" show, writes: "Body, menace, death, shit, murder … already we are able to sense the agenda of the young British artists. They are probing certain boundaries it had never occurred to us to think about" ("'Sensation' in Brooklyn," *Nation* [November 1, 1999]: 26). One rediscovers here something more than the lingua franca of the recent art scene. One rediscovers as well something like the mimesis of belief and the mimesis of publicness that is also the contemporary condition of belief, intimacy, and publicness. For what exactly does it mean to appeal to the disruption of a conventional reality whose disruption is, of course, the conventional reality? What exactly does this *no-longerism* posit, other than something like the historical sense of, say, MTV's House of Style? And what does it mean to posit that it has never occurred to "us" to think about the only things the art scene (in the faux sensation of the Sensation show, for example) has been thinking about, its clichés du jour? The point not to be missed is that this referred sensation and referred belief are here exactly the condition of sensation and belief. (And this is not merely because such clichés cannot be reduced to "mere" clichés—precisely in that the cliché is, again, the voice of the community at its purest.) For it is not quite accurate to say that the speaker of such beliefs—"disrupts our conventional expectations," "no longer simple … no longer ideal," "never occurred to us to think about," and so on—believes them. The speaker of such beliefs believes that everyone believes them. That is, he believes through the citation to others and to an elsewhere—to a public without a place. He believes, in effect, through the other, which means, by extension, that the other can believe for him. This

is the structure and appeal, for example, of "public opinion" and "popular psychology." And it is the structure of the mimesis of publicness: belief by way of the detour of believing a fiction of what *other* people *elsewhere* believe, while we may stay skeptical ourselves. The mimesis of belief cannot be separated from a sort of *collective transitivism*. That is, one believes through the opinions or feelings of *no one in particular,* through the opinion or feeling of *everyone else* that one can then cite, feel, and believe as *one's own*. Or, as Michel de Certeau puts it, "the 'real' is what, in a given place, reference to another place makes people believe in." Michel de Certeau, *The Practice of Everyday Life* (Berkeley: University of California Press, 1984), 188.

39. See, for example, Thomas Elsaesser, "Subject Positions, Speaking Positions: From *Holocaust, Our Hitler,* and *Heimat* to *Shoah* and *Schindler's List,*" in *The Persistence of History: Cinema, Television, and the Modern Event,* ed. Vivian Sobchack (New York: Routledge, 1996), 145–183.

Postscript on the Violence–Media Complex (and Other Games)

As long as we are only playing we do not cross a Rubicon——neither in war nor in love.

Eugen Fink, Spiel als Weltsymbol

We lead an indoor social life.

*Erving Goffman, The Presentation of Self in Everyday
Life*

All but war is simulation.

Corporate Logo, Illusion, Inc.

"'There's no such thing as a perfect murder,' Tom said to
Reeves," opening Patricia Highsmith's novel *Ripley's Game;*
"'That's just a parlour game.'"[1] Yet the relation between murder
and game is here a good deal more complicated—and not least
in that the murder leisure industry is premised precisely on
their paradoxical connection. The crime plotter Reeves, who
sets the novel in motion, is "like a small boy playing a game
he had invented himself, a rather obsessive game with severe
rules—for other people" (*Game*, p. 112). But the point is not
exactly that Reeves exempts himself from the rules of the game

he invents by seeing through them. The paradox, more exactly, is that obsessively playing the game and seeing through it are not at all at odds. If one does not see outside the rules, one will not play by the rules—which means that one cannot play by the rules unless one sees through them: seeing through the game is part of it.

Game or play, for one thing, might be seen as the model for reflexive modernity—or better, its self-modeling. Along these lines, it has been suggested that play "is the social phenomenon per se."[2] In play, that is, modern society is experienced as it is: in that modern society must reflect onto itself its self-constitution—its contingency, its self-conditioning, and its deliberate complication—the social construction of reality looks like the play of the world. "The paradox of play," as Dirk Baecker (following Gregory Bateson) sets out, "is that one can perform actions in play that do not mean what they mean. The bite of a playing dog is actually a pinch and not a bite, yet it stands for both the pinch and the bite. Play simulates what it dissimulates."[3] The act/play distinction, reflecting on itself, reenters the act and thus appears as the frame and condition of social action.

This is the region of true crime and its media apriori: the vague and shifting and self-reflected line between fact and fiction, act and game. And, again, to the extent that this media doubling of the world is itself seen as the perfect crime—as the murder of reality, as a crime against humanity—true crime and the media apriori double each other.

Hence play borders on the break-ins of real life—the injury, the accident, sexual excitation, violence; the violations of the boundary between players and spectators; the crossings between play and world—that at once distinguish it and impregnate it. Seeing through the game is part of it; the outside of the game—the world—thus enters into the game, the outside seen from the inside. And that means that the difference between playing by the rules and playing with the rules is in play too.

The point is not at all that the social order is a game (unless one misunderstands the social construction of reality as play—and thus suspends belief in the reality of social construction). The real point is that to the extent that modernity is defined by its contingency, self-conditioning, and deliberate complication, it must operate via a paradoxical self-exposure.

Here it becomes possible to see why modern social conditions cannot work if they are *not* self-exposing.[4]

In modern parlor games like the perfect murder story, false or true, make-believe makes belief. Tom Ripley, we are told, "believed in positive thinking" (*Game,* p. 119). That is, Tom believed in belief—and hence in the mass circulation and media credibility of such best-selling things as "the power of positive thinking." That indoor world, grounded in nothing deeper than itself, is marked by a reflexivity without reserve—and the knowledge of that.

This makes for a sociology of half-credences, counterfactual life, and everyday brinksmanship, for example, the sociology of Highsmith's contemporary Erving Goffman, with its cold war of everyday life—with all its communication contingencies, interaction rituals, and pseudo-*gemeinschaft* of mass-simulated intimacy (as the alternative to mass and media both). On the logic of this stranger-intimacy and cold sociality, for example, "there is, then, a statistical relation between appearances and reality, not an intrinsic or necessary one."[5] Or (as Deleuze and Guattari express it), "there is always something statistical in our loves."[6]

Here it becomes possible to see too that the locked room of true and false crime is a scale model of the sequestration of society, of the modern social condition: "The wing of the hospital where Jonathan had to go looked like a laboratory of the future ... a seemingly endless corridor of sound-proofed floor surface" (*Game,* p. 59). Jonathan—terminally ill, periodically having his blood recycled, subject to the calculus of risk, to the relays of bodies and information, to social life-support systems—is the modern individual enclosed in a corridor-world, the subject proper to Ripley's cold war games, par excellence.

This is the individual who does not know who he is, since he must decide the issue for himself: he winds himself up to see where he goes. And this is at once the freedom and the terror of a self-induced and self-corroborated social life. That freedom and that terror—both premised on the individual who makes himself from himself in the world order that makes itself from itself—is nowhere more evident, more lurid or more lethal or more game-like, than in the border genres of true and false crime.

The motive for Ripley's own lethal game is a too-knowing word at an accidental meeting: "Oh yes. I've heard of you" (*Game,* p. 10). Hearsay, a form of secondhand nonexperience, is the idiom of this unremitting reflexivity. It "oil[s] the machinery of social intercourse" (p. 27), which communicates nothing but its ongoing communication: "the word did get around" (p. 23). It is a world of second thoughts and "double-think" (p. 233). And its lines are drawn via a closed circuit of realization and self-realization, the recycling of blood, thoughts, beliefs, and stories. On the logic of this "cycle of disbelief to belief"[7] and back, belief and motive form an endless loop, doubling back on themselves; hence it simply "was a matter of protecting—what had gone before" (p. 228).

If an individual in the modern sense is one who observes his or her own observing, then "whoever fails to understand this intuitively or is not made aware of this by his or her therapist can read novels and project them onto the self."[8] One sees too, then, what cannot be seen, without the possibility of getting behind it: "What did the back of a glass eye look like?" (*Game,* p. 151). The players in this world are thus addicts of the secondary—an addiction to the secondary answerable less to the archaeology of knowledge than to an archaeology of knowingness.

The inventory of the conditions of modern violence in *Ripley's Game* thus includes true crime as part of its fiction. The game, like that of Sartre's waiter pretending to be a waiter, "is a kind of marking out and investigation"—a trying out of the world "in order to realize it."[9]

Jonathan reads true crime—the book supplied by Reeves, along with a gun—as precrime: "the book was called *The Grim Reapers: The Anatomy of Organized Crime in America.* ... The book held facts, after all, and the facts were fascinating" (*Game,* pp. 86–87). And yet in Highsmith's overexposed and self-realizing world of "story, fact, counterfact," there are these "Mafiosi—that charming, squabbling batch of families which the Italian-American League claimed did not exist, claimed were a figment of fiction-writers' imagination. Why, the church itself with its bishops making blood liquefy at the festival of San Gennaro ... all *this* was more real than the Mafia!" (p. 112). Transubstantiation, on the logic of these system-specific comparative realisms, is more real than the turning of fiction into fact, more real than "reading *The Godfather* again" (p. 91).

This is not, or not simply, a matter of bourgeois interiority once again chasing its own tail; nor is it a matter covered, simply, by the pseudonym "postmodernism" (itself an indication of where the embarrassment in periodizing something like "modernism" leads—scenes of reading and writing, the media apriori). It marks, we have seen, the presumption that the question of criminality and the question of the media are two sides of the same formation, one that works as a system. It marks, that is, the conditions of action in modern social systems: the "departments into which the doing of actions is organized ... the specific stages[s] in the machinery of action"—including their stage machinery.[10] Social action is subjected to its self-corroboration and evaluation, "to the contingency of being under the observation of others," and is rereflected in "the manufacture and distribution of vicarious experience through the mass media"—the presumption of the media apriori in a jointly sustained and, therefore, known world.[11]

In Highsmith's *Strangers on a Train,* Guy Haines's murder weapon is a gun he had bought years before, bought "not because it was a gun but because it was beautiful." Yet this is not exactly an aestheticization of murder, as one of the fine arts. We are told further, and with a striking gratuitousness, that he had "bought it with money from his paper route."[12] The commutability of the paper route and the gun is not at all surprising in a novel about vicarious crimes and surrogate sensualities, about substitution or representation not as the *alternative* to face-to-face acts of violence but as the *motive* for them. These are elementary particles of the crime system and its modus operandi from the start. The crucial point is that the commutability of gun and paper route has its place in the more general matrix of communication and commuting that make up the psychotechnologies of everyday life. As Norbert Wiener, the founder of cybernetics, expressed it some time ago, both persons and machines are, above all, communicative organisms: "the distinction between material transportation [bodies, matter] and message transportation [bits of information] is not in any theoretical sense permanent or unbridgeable."[13] As systems theorist Niklas Luhmann more recently, and equally dispassionately, summarizes it: "The system of society consists of communications. There are no other elements, no further substance than communications."[14]

Body processing and information processing—matter and message transport and their coordination—are the story of true crime, and its fictional codependents. In Highsmith's *Those Who Walk Away,* that coupling of matter and message transport is intensified to the point where the communicative infrastructure of this world becomes visible. This is a gamelike world (a cat-and-mouse game) that lays bare the violence–media complex. The characters, stalking each other, "watched the papers daily, morning and evening":

> "What's in the paper?" Inez asked. "Let's have some coffee, dear." Coleman gestured to the tray on the writing-table. ... "Nothing about where he is. In the paper?" "No, just a report he's missing. I wish I'd thought to order orange juice." ... Inez brought Coleman his coffee, she picked up the telephone and ordered two orange juices and asked if she could have a *Gazzettino*. ... "Wait till I see the paper. I'll speak with them if I have to." The paper and the orange juice arrived. Garrett's picture, probably his passport picture, was one-column wide on the front page, and the item below it was some two inches long. (*Those Who*, pp. 106–107)

Message and matter (papers and juice cans) circulate together (and the materiality of the media—measured in inches, columns, pages—insists here too). The city, we know, is a system for moving people, food, water, energy, money, waste, and information. That social system is what silently runs, as the known world's infrastructure—and the crime system italicizes the media apriori, such that violence, as the sending of a message, is communication by other means.

In the closely watched world of referred belief and referred experience, surveillance, for example, is generalized as a new kind of togetherness. William Saroyan, the "writer in residence" for an early version of reality TV, *Candid Camera,* put it in these terms: the reality show "shows people who don't know they're being watched. And that's the essence of drama, isn't it."[15] On this account, the TV viewer is in effect in the position of true and false crime's self-reading reader, the viewer or reader who—like the detective or the psychiatrist or, until recently, God—cannot merely "observe the unobserved observer"[16] but, beyond that, is able to see what others cannot see and see that they cannot see that.

How people act and observe when they cannot observe their observation is part of the cold war years' intensification of the mass pedagogy in media reflection and self-reflection. (It might be recalled that one of the leading social observers of those years, David Riesman, called *Candid Camera*'s creator, Allen Funt, "The second most ingenious sociologist in America." I have been sampling Goffman's accounts of second-order observation as well.) Saroyan's job, as writer in residence for a candid television show, was, more precisely, to script sketches for actors to perform. Funt would then try to duplicate, or to realize, the social situations Saroyan scripted via the spontaneous interactions with people on the street, people just like you and me. Or, as *Newsweek* concisely expressed it, the point of comparing these rival modes of presentation was "to compare reality and fiction."[17]

The comparison of real and fictional reality, as collective pedagogy, is thus at the same time a redrawing of the boundaries between public and private reality in terms of the media doubling of the world (the mechanical doubling of act and observation). The current interest or fascination with utterly exposed or "bare" life is, at least in part, a fascination with the stripping away of social forms (forms of communication) as a way of seeing and touching the real. There is no doubt a dubious ethics to the witnessing of exposed life, from reality TV to atrocity exhibitions (and this no doubt makes for its relentless—and relentlessly paradoxicalized—ethicization). But it is also a continuation, at least in part, of the interest in the everyday openness of everyone, a continuation of the interest, from the later eighteenth century on, in synthetic witnessing as the social bond.

These paradoxes of stranger-intimacy are nowhere more in evidence than in the intensification of social self-reflection called reality TV. The interest of reality TV is not the universalization of observation (whether seen as modeling democratic transparency or as the mutation of Big-Brotherism from invasion to entertainment). The real interest of reality TV is how it makes the unobservability of this universalized observation visible—and then reinvisibilizes it. The paradox of public intimacy is that one must observe how a person observes without observers—and how one learns to ignore the paradoxes on both sides of this scene and to try out the ways of at once exposing and ignoring that situation.[18]

Consider (following Luhmann's accounts of "love as passion" and the "codification of intimacy") the styles of observing communication, or observing its unobservability, in the courtship reality shows. Men and women speak to each other in a nakedly transparent idiom of frank and open self-declaration—which cannot avoid, of course, sounding just like what frank and open self-declaration is supposed to sound like. This is an idiom of sincere self-disclosure that necessarily lays bare the paradoxes always at work in communicating sincerity; one cannot, of course, in announcing one's sincerity, avoid evoking reverse-effects and provoking suspicion.

Consider, too, the voice-overs that structure such confessional moments. It is not merely that these voice-overs are often assisted by imbedded media-within-media forms and thus immediately refer intimacy to a media rivalry, such that they become two ways of saying the same thing. (Imbedded media are hardwired to love games and war games both.) These voice-overs are nothing but *soliloquies* by which a character speaks the truth of her heart out loud. But the soliloquy by which one speaks one's interior—and speaks primarily about speaking one's interior or, more often, about knowing that one does not know it—has the same paradoxical structure for others. That is, it is invisible and unheard by other characters while visible and overheard by a mass audience. And that mass audience sees and hears too what others on stage with her cannot see or hear and, beyond that, what she herself cannot hear or observe in what she says.

Hence the romance of these shows is not protected by the pretense that these characters fail to observe that they are being observed, that they self-observe as if unobserved (making the nonobservation of this observation visible). The one thing proscribed is direct reference to that, since knowingness consists, in the paradox of public intimacy, of ignoring its existence. Nor is the romance of these shows simply "romance" in that one cannot do away with the suspicion that the characters are acting or acting themselves rather than really performing acts, that even their unscripted moments are intentionally unintentional. The real romance is that, however transparent these paradoxes of sincerity and spontaneity become, the observed romance seems to work for the observed anyway. And it works for the observer too, whether she "sees through" these intimacies or identifies with them, reflects on what one cannot see, or reflects on that reflexivity. We know, from novels and films and songs, that true love—"true romance"—is bound up through and through with the mass media, as the unconscious of the unconscious. But if we know then the artificiality of true romance, we know too, then, from the same novels and films and songs, that true love conquers all, including that artificiality.

The same goes for today's violence games or war games. Both modern love and modern war spectacularize themselves. This makes for the deep suspicion about the sincerity, or reality, of both. The vague and shifting line between true and false romance and between true and false crime means that there is no way of knowing for certain when or if one has crossed the Rubicon of love and war, not least in that the social field (its self-generation and self-corroboration) consists in the ongoing redrawing of those lines—with all the half-credences that involves.

This is nowhere more evident than in recent versions of the media doubling of violence. I am referring to contemporary variants—from reality show violence to war games—of what might be described as localizations of the violence–media complex.[19]

These games, like *Candid Camera,* compare fiction and reality. And, in the self-programming and self-running of these counterfactual realities (the media "ring"), media and violence are imbedded in each other. The war games that proliferated during the cold war years were, as one RAND analyst put it, "a technique for creating synthetic experience."[20] As one commentator in the Office of the Joint Chiefs of Staff expressed it, in 1964, during the first public discussion of war gaming: "I'm afraid that before I finish, you will associate our efforts more with those of Cecil B. DeMille than [the mathematician and systems theorist] John Von Neumann."[21] The worldly imperative of this "serious play" made for comparative realisms. Hence during the war gaming of the Cuban missile crisis, one gamer responded to the comment that "this crisis sure demonstrates how realistic Schelling's games are" with: "No, Schelling's games demonstrate how unrealistic this Cuban crisis is."[22] These modelings of synthetic experience are part of what one historian of this way of "simulating the unthinkable" has called the cold war *avant garde.*[23] Or, as Jonathan puts it in *Ripley's Game*, "Jonathan didn't believe it was entirely a game … [he] stopped thinking about that possibility. Unthinkable" (*Game*, p. 189).

There is a long history to these modern war games, from the *Kreigspielen* of the 1880s on.[24] (From then on, the two sides of the game are color-coded red and blue. The red states/blue states thing has its origin in war games: electoral politics as war games by other means.) "Embedded journalism" is only one of the self-scandalizing symptoms then of the reentry of the media apriori in modern violence.

This should by now be familiar enough. If reflexivity is the central problem of modernity, then one can scarcely claim a self-exemption from it by reflecting on it. If the media apriori determines our social and intimate conditions, then communicating about communication via communication scarcely exempts us from it either. (Exposing reflexivity is not like exposing a secret or even detecting an open one. The self-exposing character of the media is part of how it works.)[25]

The media, from writing and print on, develop possibilities of social communication (social relation) without interaction: the psychotechnologies of everyday life that make up our situation. To the extent that this is experienced as a crime against humanity, violence (and its synthetic witnessing) will, paradoxically enough, be solicited as its antidote—as if the problem with war were not that it is murderous but that it is mediated. This amounts to the solicitation of violence as an alternative to the media apriori (*Welcome to the desert of the real!*). The direct binding of violence and media is represented exactly in reverse (*All but war is simulation!*). This "violence as the antidote to simulation" in effect sanctions wounding as a return to the real. One sign of that is the contemporary (popular and academic) culture of the wound: traumatophilia and the burgeoning of proxy witnessing and referred mourning. That's why, as J. G. Ballard puts it in his recent novel *Super-Cannes*, "in this millennium their great dream is to become victims."[26]

Notes

1. Patricia Highsmith, *Ripley's Game* (1974; London: Vintage, 1999), 5; subsequent references hereafter abbreviated *Game* in parentheses within text.
2. Dirk Baecker, "The Form Game," in *Problems of Form*, ed. Dirk Baecker (Stanford, CA: Stanford University Press, 1999), 102.

3. Baecker, "The Form Game," 105.

4. This means that the notion of "simulation" does not take us very far in unpacking this paradox. The paradox of play can only proceed by reflecting onto itself that "this is a play"—and then ignoring it. The distinction that founds play ruins it in becoming explicit once the game is in motion. The games people play—the forms of make-believe or half- belief that, we have seen, reflect the paradox of modern sociality and its media apriori—mean that the difference between playing by the rules and playing with the rules is in play too. On paradoxical relation of rules and fiction, I am indebted to Roger Caillos, *Man, Play, and Games* (New York: Schocken Books, 1961). See also Jesper Juul, *Half-Real: Video Games between Real Rules and Fictional Worlds* (Cambridge, MA: MIT Press, 2005).

5. Erving Goffman, *The Presentation of Self in Everyday Life* (New York: Doubleday, 1959), 71.

6. Gilles Deleuze and Félix Guattari, *Anti-Oedipus: Capitalism and Schizophrenia,* trans. Robert Hurley, Mark Seem, and Helen R. Hunt (Minneapolis: University of Minnesota Press, 1983), 105.

7. Goffman, *The Presentation of Self in Everyday Life,* 20.

8. Niklas Luhmann, *Observations on Modernity,* trans. William Whobrey (Stanford, CA: Stanford University Press, 1998), 7.

9. Jean-Paul Sartre, *Being and Nothingness,* trans. Hazel E. Barnes (New York: Philosophical Library, 1956), 59.

10. Erving Goffman, *Interaction Ritual: Essays on Face-to Face Behavior* (New York: Pantheon, 1967), 217, quoting J. L. Austin, "Plea for Excuses" (Philosophical Papers, ed. J. Urmson and G. Warnock [Oxford: Oxford University Press, 1961]), 141.

11. Goffman, *Interaction Ritual,* 226, 262.

12. Patricia Highsmith, *Strangers on a Train* (New York: Penguin, 1950), 113.

13. Norbert Wiener, *The Human Use of Human Beings: Cybernetics and Society* (Garden City, NJ: Doubleday, 1954), 136.

14. Niklas Luhmann, "Modes of Communication and Society," in *Essays on Self-Reference* (New York: Columbia University Press, 1990), 99–106.

15. Quoted in Anna McCarthy, "Stanley Milgram, Allen Funt, and Me," in *Reality TV: Remaking Television Culture,* ed. Susan Murray and Laurie Ouellette (New York: New York University Press, 2004), 28.

16. Goffman, *The Presentation of Self in Everyday Life,* 7.

17. "Time of His Life," *Newsweek* (September 10, 1962): 94.

18. For a related account, see Niklas Luhmann, "The Evolutionary Differentiation between Society and Interaction," in *The Micro-Macro Link,* ed. Jeffrey C. Alexander, Bernhard Giesen, Richard Munch, and Neil J. Smelser

(Berkeley: University of California Press, 1987), 112–131; see also *Differentiation Theory and Social Change: Comparative and Historical Perspectives,* ed. Jeffrey C. Alexander and Paul Colomy (New York: Columbia University Press, 1990).

19. See Timothy Lenoir, "All but War Is Simulation: The Military-Entertainment Complex," *Configurations* 8 (2000): 238–335.

20. See Sharon Ghamari-Tabrizi, "Simulating the Unthinkable: Gaming Future War in the 1950s and 1960s," *Social Studies of Science* 30, no. 2 (April 2000): 193.

21. Ghamari-Tabrizi, "Simulating the Unthinkable," 191.

22. Ghamari-Tabrizi, "Simulating the Unthinkable," 213.

23. Ghamari-Tabrizi, "Simulating the Unthinkable," 170. See also Sharon Ghamari-Tabrizi, *The Worlds of Herman Kahn: The Intuitive Science of Thermonuclear War* (Cambridge, MA: Harvard University Press, 2005). As Ghamari-Tabrizi observes, "Setting the terms for gaming and man-machine simulations in the 1950s and later, RAND analysts commended these techniques for sharpening intuition, stimulating creativity, offering insight into complex fields of interaction, exploring intersubjective exchanges in an interdisciplinary research setting, instilling tolerance for ambiguity and uncertainty, and heightening sensitivity to the practioners' own blindspots and rigidities" (Ghamari-Tabrizi, *The Worlds of Herman Kahn,* 170). Here one finds precisely what will define the "New Criticism's" better living through ambiguity—and what will anticipate a deconstructive "cultural studies" outlook appropriate to a social and intellectual program heading toward diversity and an idiom of "contested terrains" and radical "openness." Such a coincidence of techniques hesitates as well the continuing assumption that diversity or heterogeneity is the antidote to a "monolithic" model of power. This is the case not merely in the solicitation of a proliferation of desires, individualities, and intensities in contemporary consumer and self-design culture: modern social systems cease to function if foreclosed. No doubt the colonizing of the future, in the operation of the risk society, and the emphasis on the "reentry" of the system into the system, in systems theory, provide renovated models of the uses and abuses of uncertainty. But they indicate, at the same time, that a default politics based on diversity, proliferation, and openness misses these renovations and their modus operandi.

24. General H. Norman Schwarzkopf recounts this version of the game—here called "Internal Look"!— played during the first Iraq war, in his memoir *It Doesn't Take a Hero:* "We played Internal Look in late July 1990, setting up a mock headquarters complete with computers and communication

gear at Eglin Air Force Base in the Florida panhandle. As the exercise got under way, the movements of Iraq's real-world ground and air forces eerily paralleled the imaginary scenario of the game. … As the war game began, the message center also passed along routine intelligence bulletins about the real Middle East. Those concerning Iraq were so similar to the game dispatches that the message center ended up having to stamp the fictional reports with a prominent disclaimer, 'Exercise Only.'" The uncanniness, or half-credence, here registered in the coincidence of real and fictional reality becomes second nature in more recent war games. The counterfactual realities of the game are progressively incorporated into it: for example, in accounts of developing "believable agents" in modeling the games; in the programming of "soft characteristics" into the game such that they include "time-line based experiences of how individuals felt, thought and reacted to the dynamic unfolding of events—their fears and emotions as well as actions"; and, perhaps above all, the introduction of "interactive, predictive, operational simulation." By the second Iraq war, simulation units "could be reduced and actually embedded into M1 tank units, attack helicopters, or F16s," such that an "ongoing comparison" of real and fictional reality reenters the battlefield itself.

25. The contemporary stalling of a politically interested theory between the "too late" (trauma) and the "too soon" (messianism) is one sign of that. So too is running up the white flag of "ethics"—as if ethics (the self-reflection of morality) were the antidote to an unremitting reflexivity. And that ethics, in any case, is "covered" by its impossibility ("the perpetual illusion of morality") and by its undecidable and "pure contingency" and "pure, absolute potentiality"—as if contingency were not the defining attribute of modernity. I am here quoting and sampling Giorgio Agamben ("Bartleby, or On Contingency," in *Potentialities: Collected Essays in Philosophy,* ed. and trans. Daniel Heller-Roazen [Stanford, CA: Stanford University Press, 1999], 243–277). In his account of Bartleby as a figure of pure, absolute potentiality, for example, Agamben transforms that pure contingency into "a paradigm for literary writing" (p. 260). That account is therefore remarkably—that is, programmatically—inattentive to the forms of writing, posting, and communication that structure Melville's story—which is thus taken to communicate nothing but its noncommunicativeness (its pure literariness).

26. J. G. Ballard, *Super-Cannes* (London: Flamingo, 2001), 365.

Index